Table of Contents

FOREWORD

Five years ago, my dear uncle Tiago took the fateful leap into the unknown; but this wasn't the first time he'd faced death – in fact I'm sure he danced with it more times than most. A quote always comes to mind, one that I believe resonates with his story and is ironically from a film depicting the lives of two racers - (RUSH): *"The closer you are to death, the more alive you feel. It's a wonderful way to live. It's the only way to drive."* Despite the physical impairments he carried throughout his life, he still flew valiantly without brakes nor fear through the adversity that might have kept most people down. Those that knew him would agree that he definitely shared this philosophy with the character in the film. *"My life could be a movie"*, said by him, and many others who knew his story.

The most recent time I was in Brazil, would unknowingly be the last time I would get to spend time with my "crazy" uncle. The older you get the more aware you become of the people around you, who they are, where they've been, what they've seen. I always remember having a great time with Tiago growing up, he happened to be living in London at the time I was born, which I guess forged a connection between us before I could comprehend one. This time in 2014, I was in my mid 20's and still quite late in my maturity. I think that this is one of the traits myself and Tiago had in common. Having had regular contact with him despite the distance, he was a guide for me throughout my rebellious years. I am now certain that he – being rebellious in nature himself – was using his experience to teach me how to channel my energy towards a place of balance. In the two weeks I would spend in Rio, I was fortunate enough to spend many precious moments with

Tiago, we connected on a much deeper level than ever before. Taking me around this magical place, we trekked up mountains, watched sunrises and flew above the city. Everywhere we went he was greeted with such warmth, whether it be in a small cafe getting some post-flight frozen açai, or by his comrades in flight; everyone knew Tiago Cobra. Behind the adrenaline-fueled man, was a very centered and spiritual being. Someone that liked to climb the highest mountains, to then jump off them and fly at insane speeds – but would ensure that he'd reach the summit just as the sun was creeping over the horizon. Here is where he found his peace, between the clouds and the infinite, away from societal demands and the conflicting disharmony of the world below. So high that the air carried with it nothing but the reverberate sound of nature, a place to truly balance himself before pushing the boundaries of human limitation.

I have him to thank for where I am today. He gave me love and motivation at a time where I was lost. He taught me that it is ok to fail - because to fail is to learn and being aware of this helped me understand ego. Teaching me about the power of the mind, how it – with love and good intention – can be applied to shape your reality and change the world around you. I was lucky to have known him for the first 24 years of my life, and will carry his wisdom with me until I too have fulfilled my purpose here. With the help of my grandfather Francisco Amorim, writer of this book that I have had the honor of translating, and all of our family and friends, we will tell this story to share the limitless inspiration that was him, and his life.

INTRODUCTION

Losing a son so young, at the tender age of 17, left a void that could never be filled and a pain that would never heal. He was intelligent, with great skill in music and a talent for mechanics, loved philosophy, had many friends and was healthy. Time, the great remedy, it helps to carry the suffering, more so when a parent's life is riddled with problems – problems that go beyond one's professional occupation, beyond a war, a relocation to a new country where everything had to start again, from square one.

Then to lose another son forty-two years later; this one at the age of 47. He was as bright as his eldest brother, with the same talent for music and mechanics, born into an unexpected life of suffering which he lived through laughing, turning his pain to humor. Now, his mother and I are over 80 years old, and the time left is insufficient to help suppress the pain once more.

It wasn't easy gathering all the words to write a short story of a person's passage through life, who unlike many, made friends who admired him everywhere he went. Let alone for a father, who during the search for testimonies and all of the available documents, in all the pages I would write, shed many tears of longing and tenderness. Mixed with a feeling of guilt for not giving my children, not only this one but all, the love that they always deserved.

In some passages tears were mixed with laughter. Apparently, he just couldn't let it be. Tiago, even in the most dramatic and painful moments of his life, smiled at everyone, and with his skills, his conversations and good mood, always brought a good energy to any place he was in. It seems he was born philosophizing! He studied very little as a child and throughout his teenage years, but he was profound in the few notes and letters he has left us.

Like his older brother Jorge, who died when Tiago was just 5, he always dreamt of leading a more spiritual life, with love and peace being the core of living. While Jorge had gone through hypnotic experiences, reported in a letter written by him at the age of sixteen, Tiago, when already a man, took a short course to study that same technique. Both born into Christianity, they distanced themselves from the church due to its stifling bureaucracy, incomprehensible liturgy and pompous golden clothing. They both didn't completely depart from Christ, but they dreamed of a religion that was more humble, a mixture of Christianity and Buddhism, as Tiago later wrote.

Jorge never did have time to affirm himself. Tiago, on the other hand, was able to live according to his conscience, always cheerful, with a good disposition that was contagious to whomever spent time with him. Always looking for what was beyond the horizon, he glided through life with an open heart, magnetizing countless friends his way, who loved and respected him as he went. In speed he found freedom, a discharge for his energy. He lived running, it seemed that nothing could satisfy his need – first on a bicycle, then a motorbike, a car, until finally he found speed in the skies. This would be the ultimate race, against the elements and himself. Forever chasing that release of adrenaline.

Nobody knows how much they will miss someone until they are gone. It is impossible to measure each one's pain. As much as we think of all his adventures, many of them crazy beyond belief, and his ability to make everyone happy with his amazing energy. The loss of a child is a pain that can never be cured. Let alone two.

The idea of gathering some passages from his life into this small book, is to offer it to those who loved him, respected him and lived with him – remembering some questions that he asked himself inside:

"What is most important in life?
Material well-being or freedom? It is difficult to separate one from the other.
You may ask yourself: what is the use of being rich without freedom? Will not the poor but free person be happier?"

THE FAMILY

I married my wife Gabriela in Lisbon, Portugal in 1954. We were both well brought up, by parents and ancestors who taught us respect. From this, grew a deep sense of duty and ethics. As soon as we married, we left to live in the City of Luanda, Angola, to start our new life.

The following year we returned to Lisbon. I then went back to Angola in 1956, and the family would reunite in Africa again in 1957. Now double the size, with two young children, the first born was Jorge, in Lisbon 1955. Then came Luis, who was born in '57 in the same city. The others were all born in Luanda thereafter: Francisco (Chico) was born in 1958, Helena '60, João '61, Joana '64, Tiago '67 and finally Lourenço in 1970. Hence the deep connection that everyone in the family feels for Angola as well as for Mozambique, where we lived for just over three years.

Some of them were quieter, others more agitated. Tiago was like a bee that flew, run without stopping, always chasing after something.

Christmas 1970 (Gabriela with all the brothers and sisters in Luanda with the new born Lourenco)

1967 - LUANDA

On November 7th, the seventh and penultimate child was born. Tiago, coming into an already large family where turmoil reigned from the agitation of the older siblings, was still received with the same joy as always.

It is of this son, and to a lesser extent the eldest, that we will talk about in this book. It will be very difficult to write this little story, of a human being who from such a young age showed the greatness of his soul, and the determination to live his life in his own way. These characteristics had already been demonstrated by his eldest brother who was with us for such a short time.

At the time, the cost of his birth was 3,756 escudos (about $160 US Dollars) at the clinic. Shortly thereafter he was baptized in the *Sagrada Família* Church, in Luanda, close to the family home. He was given the name Tiago de Almeida Gomes de Amorim.

After his baptism he was blessed once more by a great family friend, Cónego Eduardo André Muaca, a native of Cabinda, who later became the Archbishop of Luanda. He always wore an impeccably well-kept white cassock that contrasted strikingly with his dark skin. He often came to visit the family home, the children called him "Uncle Muaca", they would sit on his lap, and he always felt comfortable with the "nephews" & "nieces". A great friendship was forged with this gentleman, and everyone felt a deep sense of admiration for him.

Tiago's godfather was to be his eldest brother, Jorge. Cousin Zeza Gaivão was chosen to be godmother, and by proxy, Aunt Isabel Perestrello.

Tiago started walking at an early age. At 8 months old, he quickly began to produce signs of concern because he could not stay still or quiet. He was excited, very excited in fact, and always with a beautiful smile on his face – constantly surrounded by the affection of his brothers and sisters. After him, the eighth and final sibling was born.

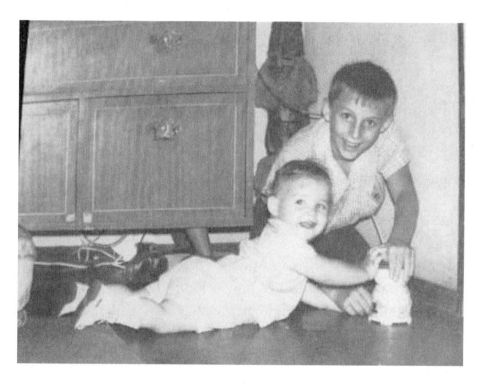

1 year old Tiago with brother Chico. Always with some injury on his body. Look at his forehead!

1970 - 1975: THE BEGINNING OF HIS ADVENTURES

His first "big" adventure was on April 21st 1970. It was to be his first flight, and at just 2 and a half years old at the time. Being the curious baby that he was, he wanted to look outside of the window in the upstairs bedroom. He leant out a bit too far and carelessly fell on to a metallic wire frame that held a leafy purple bush called the 'bougainvillea bush', that shaded the cars. This particularly unpleasant shrub sprouts large, tough thorns.

The house next door was the headquarters of a Militarized Volunteer Group – men who had lost almost everything at the beginning of the terrorism in Angola. One of these neighbours saw Tiago falling and ran to get him off the thorny vines, getting scratched all over himself in the process. Tiago on the other hand, sitting scratched and hurt on top of all those spikes, cried until he was lifted out, and then proceeded to laugh!

Around the time of the first flight

It's possible that the interest in his neighbours arose when at the age of two, he spent Christmas at the *Casa dos Rapazes* Orphanage in Luanda. An institution funded by donations that took care of 160 young boys. The work was directed by Father Francisco Freitas, who became a great friend of the family. Tiago was only small but he still played with all the children. Together with his siblings, he sat among the many children on numerous occasions to enjoy Christmas dinners together.

In 1970, the last year that we lived in Luanda before moving the family to Mozambique, all 160 Christmas presents were wrapped in our house, tagged with the names of each child and given to them after a huge dinner, with everyone joining in. They were always great parties with all the children gathered together.

In 1971 the family moved to *Lourenço Marques*, capital of Mozambique, today called Maputo. In this city there was no place quite like '*Casa dos Rapazes*', but a similar foundation called the *Obra da Rua - Casa do Gaiato (Road works - The Young boys House)*, that housed, fed and educated one hundred Mozambican boys, most of whom had lost, or been abandoned by their parents. We visited the institution and offered the person in charge, Father José Maria, our support in any way. For three consecutive years we spent our Christmas nights there.

When Tiago was 5 years old, the doctor said that he needed to have an operation on his tonsils, so off we went to the clinic. Shortly before the operation, a nurse came to give him an injection to calm him down. As soon as the nurse entered the room, syringe in hand, Tiago realizing that he was going to be pricked, left that room running. He sprinted down the halls of that clinic as if he had swallowed a jet engine, with two or three nurses on his tail. He caused a tremendous stir in a place that was usually very quiet. After they caught him and calmed him down, the operation went smoothly and they returned him to us asleep. In his sleep he would occasionally make huge leaps from the hospital bed, as if violently driven up by a strong spring. I had to hold him tightly to the bed to keep him from flying out, whilst whispering very quietly into his ear: "*Calm down Tiago, it's your Dad here, I am with you*".

In 1974, the family moved back to Luanda immediately after the Carnation Revolution of 25th April 1974 – which had put an end to the colonial era. The house where the Orphanage had formerly been was now occupied by the command of the FNLA, a group of Congolese fighters who had fought against colonialism. They

14

intended to integrate the large northern portion of Angolan territory with the former Belgian Congo. Tiago, not even 5 years old, blonde haired and always free spirited, soon had free entry to that barracks full of Africans who traditionally hated whites for obvious reasons. After having won the sympathy of all those who served there, he moved freely in that generally hostile environment.

When Tiago turned 5, he started going school. One day when he returned home for lunch, he breathlessly came running in extremely excited, saying: *"Dad, Dad, I already know how to write my name!"*. He got a sheet of paper and a pen and wrote, very slowly, in a child's handwriting: O G A I T. When we saw what he'd written, we all burst out laughing, *"only something like that could come from Tiago's head"*. So, we asked him to spell it out. First letter: O, second: G, etc., and then *"read it again"*. And he exclaimed, every time, with pure confidence, *"TI-A-GO"*. No matter how many attempts we made, he insisted on writing the name backwards. No one had ever heard of dyslexia at that time, no teacher even knew what it was, and we simply attributed it to the quirk of a boy who was always running around, excited and tireless.

Much later, already in Brazil at this point, we learned that the problem was in fact dyslexia. Not only did we find out that people with dyslexic typically have an IQ above average, but that also in this period of time it was very difficult to find someone qualified to deal with this disorder. As he grew up and his mind developed, it was confirmed that his aversion to studying was the result of his dyslexia, but also that his intelligence was well above the average of his friends. Predictably, he had a hard time concentrating on his studies, which left him with low grades.

One day we gave him a simple children's book to try and read. Still in the middle of the first page, Tiago was sweating with the immense effort that it required for him to read. During his life he managed to overcome his lack of education with his willingness to discuss, research and retain knowledge.

The second stay in Luanda was short-lived, with independence looming, life became unbearable with the whistling of bullets over our house and the scarcity of food. The prospects of a future for white people there were bleak. The Portuguese traitors, who negotiated the surrender of the territories, concluded that the only representatives of the colonial territories (or overseas provinces) were those with native heritage. The whites *"could even be shot"* or *"handed over to the sharks"* according to words spoken and written by two of the mentors of the Revolution: Mário Soares and Rosa Coutinho.

The Portuguese police did nothing. Thefts and burglaries proliferated and continued. The only solution was to get out of there.

After looking for a place to relocate with seven children, we decided that the best option was to immigrate to Brazil, which opened its doors without bureaucracy. By September 1975, the whole family arrived in our new country.

1975: BRAZIL IS THE DESTINATION

The early days in Brazil were extremely difficult for us. Without work and with seven children on our backs, any chance of work had to be grabbed quickly with both hands. With the exception of Chico, who got into university to study Architecture in Niterói, the family went to live on a farm in the interior of the State of *Rio De Janeiro*. It was here that Tiago started to have contact with snakes.

One day, sitting and leaning against a tree, Tiago heard a rustling sound and thought it was a bird's nest. He looked and saw (only!) a rattlesnake passing through the dry leaves right beside him. He didn't seem to care much, he simply got up and left. At home, he told us with great calmness that he had been sat next to a snake!

At the farm. A few months before disaster.

The owner of the property we were living and working on was a crook, a swindler, totally corrupt and as you can imagine, ended up becoming a millionaire! This led to life on the farm ending quite badly, in addition to causing an ugly fight between myself and the crook. The family moved to *Rio das Ostras* with immediate effect. It was not the summer season yet so most of the houses were empty and easily rentable. The family moved into a spacious home, but with the house, came immense problems. Among these problems there was a very low water pressure. The shower was little more than a drip pan!

Another problem was the garbage collection which occurred only once a week! With countless stray cats and dogs wandering around, the household waste that was packed into plastic bags, would always end up scattered all over the street. The solution to this problem was to transform a 200litre barrel, into a kind of incinerator. Being mostly organic waste and plastic, it was difficult to set fire to. Pouring alcohol over it solved a small part of the problem.

I would always leave the house very early, before anyone woke up, but many times Tiago would have breakfast with me. Tiago was always the first to wake up among his siblings; he was an early riser, our morning rooster. He would then wake up his younger brother Lourenço and take him to school – which had a zero tolerance towards lateness. Gabriela would get up a little later, never too concerned about the schedule of the two little ones, because she would always hear them leaving home and knew that they would always arrive at school on time.

One day, now aged 8, Tiago slept a little longer than usual and decided that there was no point in going to school because they would not be allowed to enter in any case. He woke his sleeping brother Lourenço, and without saying anything to Gabriela, decided that the two of them would help with the burning of the garbage. At that time, the alcohol bottles had a small hole in the lid to release the liquid. When the bottle was squeezed, it squirted out reaching anything up to two meters in distance. They piled all the garbage together, set some paper on fire and tossed it on top of the pile. Tiago was too close when he squirted the alcohol inside the incinerator. A reflux of alcohol travelled up the liquid and set fire to the bottle, causing it to immediately explode in his hands, spreading the flames all over him. The 8-year-old boy's first reaction was to push his younger brother Lourenço away so that he wouldn't get burned. Then, with the burning fire all over his body, he ran to the outdoor shower which was intended for people to bathe in when returning from the beach. The water hardly ran. Still on fire, he ran into the house quietly, not wanting to call for his mother as he did not want to scare her. Gabriela had a feeling, a mother's instinct, something wasn't quite right. She ran to where he was and found him in the bathroom, once again was met with little running water. With the fire having melted away most of his shirt and shorts, Gabriela's only option was to put the fire out using just her hands. By this time, the fire had reached a large part of his body: his chest, neck, face, legs and hands. Once the fire was put out, it was clear to see the immense damage that had been done. They immediately rushed to the nearest hospital in *Macaé*. Tiago received emergency treatment from a doctor who claimed to be a specialist in burns and plastic surgery, but unfortunately, as it later came to our attention, he was irresponsible and ignorant. He had never treated a burn victim. The instructions he gave us and his medical staff were completely wrong: he would apply some ointment to the burnt areas and then wrap them in bandages.

Gabriela, in the face of such a horrific disaster, did not even think of her own wounds. Only later did she notice that she had also sustained severe burns on her hands, which still causes her some issues today. She left Tiago in the hospital, and on that same afternoon returned with his sister Joana to pick him up. She was convinced that they would have treated him by then, and that he would be ready to go home. They arrived to find Tiago bandaged from head to toe like a mummy, with only part of his face visible. He would have to stay hospitalized, in a treatment procedure that never existed in any medical textbook. Tiago endured exactly thirty-seven days there, during which every two or three days he would be taken to the operating room. Here they would give him yet another general anesthetic in order to be able to remove the rotten smelling bandages, that were clinging to the "rotten" flesh. It was impossible to remove the bandages without anesthetic, because it was an unbearably painful procedure for him. They would more or less clean his whole body, repeat that same incorrect procedure of covering him with an unknown and unsuitable ointment, followed by copious bandaging.

With an exhausted mother spending the whole day, and often most of the night beside her son, she would then be momentarily replaced by an exhausted father, who was desperately trying to work to maintain the household bills. Tiago was also surrounded by his brothers and sisters when they were able to visit, but this did little to ease the suffering that continued for the young boy. The scares that these inadequate nurses conjured up for us, who were merely apprentices of auxiliary students, were continual. There was only one professional nurse in that hospital, and she was English. On one particular day, a nurse appeared terrified and calling for someone from Tiago's family, the aura given off by this inexperienced and unskilled nurse, was such to make everyone believe that he had passed away. I ran to the operating room to find that she just wanted help in getting the stretcher into the room because she couldn't do it alone. Gabriela, strong as she was, could not take that kind of shock any longer and collapsed under this needless additional pressure. She was forced to finally go home and rest.

Then, from São Paulo came a great friend Madalena Melícias, who offered to spend the nights in hospital with Tiago so that Gabriela could try to recover a little. Thirty-seven days after arriving in that hospital, the doctor came to say that his patient could finally go home… but only because he was going on vacation! He said that from then on, Tiago could be treated at home. With almost his entire body still unhealed, but with the same spirit as always, it was now his parents who would continue to apply the ointment to his burns.

Another great friend of the family, António Nuno Melícias, came to fetch his wife after Tiago was discharged. After seeing the condition that Tiago was in, he called me that night with chilling words of warning: *"I am very sorry, but I must tell you that if Tiago continues this way, he will surely die. You have to consider some new, proper treatment."* A blow to my head wouldn't have stunned me as much as what my good friend had just said to me!

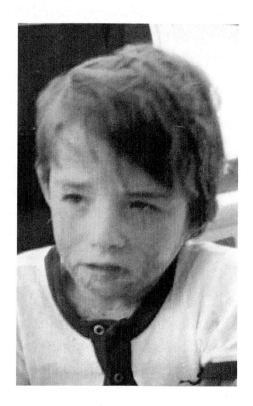

A sad 9-year-old Tiago after already having undergone some reconstructive surgery.

As parents, we remained morally strong, we had seen our child fight this disaster that had befallen him, often he'd laugh in the midst of his horrible suffering. We had been hopeful that the doctor's information that our son could go home, was purely for the reason that there was really nothing else left to do at the hospital. This friend's opinion struck like a bomb! Once again, we were devastated.

"Tomorrow morning I will return to São Paulo. I have heard that there is a hospital there that specializes in burns. I believe it to be Japanese. As soon as I arrive, I will find out and call you".

That night we received the expected phone call with the name of the place: *The Hospital of Face Defects*, on *Washington Luis Avenue*, near *Congonhas*.

That same night, I got into my car, an old Beetle, and sped to São Paulo. After circulating around for a while, a little lost in that big unknown city, I found the hospital and immediately asked to see a doctor. I explained the situation to a specialist, he told me that I could not be given an opinion without him seeing the patient. *"But, doctor, he's six hundred kilometers from here. I can't be wandering around with him looking for a hospital in his condition."*

The doctor asked some questions, one of which was whether a graft had been made. Graft was a word that was only known in medical practices. I immediately realized that the *Macaé* doctor was no more than a butcher, who should have recommended that we go to Rio, or another big city because their hospital was unable to deal with such a case. *"Doctor, I will go to pick him up now and tomorrow I will be back here."*

The doctor replied that first it was necessary to check with their reception to see if there were any vacancy. Upon enquiring, the receptionist said that there were no places! In utter desperation I told the receptionist that if I did not bring my son there, that he would surely die. She called another lady who seemed responsible for solving that kind of problem. After hearing the gravity of the situation, she told me to bring Tiago in. They would find space for him. The lady also asked if I wanted a private room, but warned of the cost that would incur. Being out of work and almost out of money, there was no way of paying for it. In the wards you didn't have to pay anything, there was also the advantage of being in contact with other patients whose help and advice could often be very important. I raced back home in my Beetle. That same night,

24

myself, Gabriela, Tiago and Lourenço made our way to *Sao Paulo*. Tiago was lying on the back seats while the floor of the car was filled with cushions to accommodate his 6-year-old brother.

Tiago entered the hospital in São Paulo at eight in the morning and went straight to the emergency room. The doctors took him and did not let us in. Shortly after, the head nurse appeared and said: *"Aren't you ashamed for having let your son get into this state?"* *"He was at the hospital in Macaé, under the care of a doctor who claimed he was a specialist! We did what he told us to do."*

The nurse looked at me in amazement, he must have cursed that doctor in his mind, but he reassured us: *"He will be fine, but the treatment will take some time."*

We left him in the hospital and returned to see him that afternoon. He was in a small ward, smiling away. The first thing he said was, *"Here they know how to treat burns. I hardly feel the pain anymore."*

And there he stayed for another month and a half, undergoing such grafts to close the burnt areas. According to doctors, the burns covered 84% of his body. Usually, people do not survive such a traumatic ordeal. According to experts, it seems that what had saved him was that he had no damage to his stomach area, but we always believed that Tiago resisted and won because he had that extraordinary inner strength and an immense will to live. He was the only child in that eight-bed ward, the rest were men.

One day, a patient came in who was crying out in agony in the middle of the night. Tiago, with immense difficulty got out of bed and went to console the man. He was just over 8 and a half years old, and already a great example for everyone. As for the man, he never screamed again.

From the very first day of the accident, Tiago's skin had turned yellow. There was not even a spot of pink on his face or lips. The blood had all been absorbed to heal the wounds that were not covered. In this new hospital they started making skin grafts: with a blade, in a kind of shaver machine, they took an extremely thin "slice" of the epidermis and covered the affected areas. A few days later, they removed skin from somewhere on his leg that had not been burned. To continue, they had to wait for the leg to regenerate in order to remove another layer. On the day of the final graft, Tiago's cheeks returned to their beautiful colour. After 90 days, the first part of the battle was won.

Once he was out of the danger zone and discharged, he looked like a little monster, like the hunchback of Nôtre Dame. His chin resting against his chest, his arms twisted, legs curled, hands deformed, in short – a horrendous spectacle, but he was alive and with his usual strength and joy. Doctors said that in the future he would have to have plastic surgery to rehabilitate the damage. However, part of the finger movements had been lost due to the wasted practices in Macaé.

1976 – 1978: SÃO PAULO

Sad and horrendous memories were created from the day Tiago first entered that hospital in Macaé, until the day he was discharged from the Hospital in São Paulo three months later. We were devastated, but happy that our son had been saved.

During that time, the family had all moved to São Paulo. When Tiago left hospital, he no longer returned to Rio das Ostras. A house was rented in Brooklin, on the Kansas Road with a courtyard overlooking the back of the landlady's house – the notorious Dona Ofélia.

Shortly after returning home, Tiago had his ninth birthday. He had recovered all of his energy, despite still being very deformed. Some friends were invited to his birthday celebrations and they all ran around the house together, excited and playing. Altogether there were about four or five at the party. Parents and uncles were present, all extremely happy to see the resourcefulness and joy in the eyes of a boy who had already suffered so much.

At ten o'clock there was an unexpected knock at the door. Gabriela went to see who it was; Dona Ofélia, complaining that after ten o'clock no noise was to be made. She wanted to rest and threatened to call the police! I asked: *"Who is there Gabriela?"* *"It's Dona Ofélia, she says that we're making a lot of noise and it's ten o'clock in the evening."* "Tell that cow not to disturb the joy of someone who has been so ill and to be gone from our lives."

Dona Ofélia must not have appreciated such comments directed at her, and soon became the family's number one enemy! The children believed her to be a witch!

Tiago and Lourenço would always play outside the house in the backyard. One day, the "evil witch" heard the children playing and absently sprayed a little water over the wall with her hose, splashing them both. Unfazed, Tiago, filled a bucket with water, went up to the floor above the storage annex, saw the lady pretending to water some flower pots, and proceeded to pour the entire bucket over the head of the "beast"!

Dona Ofélia, did you complain? No, you didn't. It was clear to see that it wasn't a good idea to mess with this family, especially Tiago! … But that wasn't the last time they would hear from Dona Ofélia.

Gabriela had taken some of the children to a fair ground, where they won some beautiful little chicks. Delighted, they took the new pets home to play with and take care of. Of course, they were well on their way to becoming chickens, with no malice intention of twisting their necks one day. The witch took advantage of the situation and complained to the City Hall that the neighbours were raising chickens at home, which was prohibited within the city.

Following the complaint, inspectors appeared and saw the four chicks! Each one still had some of their baby feathers, each of different colours. The inspectors felt terrible but had to do their duty and the children had to give up the chicks who were later eaten. The "love" for the witch grew stronger, but I do not have any memories of how they continued to "return such kindness".

On January 17, 1977, the reconstructive plastic surgeries began. Always under general anesthetic, they first lifted skin from Tiago's right shoulder. Then on the 26th, a new intervention was made for the reconstruction of the neck: placing skin from the shoulder onto the neck. He left the hospital on February 8th, and had to return every two days to reapply the dressing.

March 30th and 31st, it was back to the hospital again. This time they lifted the skin from the left shoulder, and replaced the skin on the left side of his neck. He was discharged on April 11th, appearing again every other day. Finally, on the 19th they removed the stitches but continued with bandages.

Now at *Brigadeiro* Hospital, on July 12th he was due to be operated on the following day. This time on the nerves in the curve of his right leg. On the 15th began rectification of the same leg, which no longer stretched properly. The tightness of the healed burnt skin had no give, and growing young boy it restricted his natural growth. On the 19th, an operation began on the right arm nerve, which had also shrunk due to growth issues. He left there on the 10th of August. At this point he had spent more than 62 days hospitalized for these operations, not including the countless times he had to go to the hospital to change the dressings!

Still living in the same house, incidents followed. One afternoon, Tiago aged 9 and Lourenço now aged 7, were seen sneaking upstairs suspiciously. Much to the boys bad luck, the stairs were directly in front of the sofa in the living room, where me and Gabriela just so happened to be sat. The boys body language said it all, shrinking into themselves as if it might have prevented them from being seen, but it caught my attention:

- *"Where are you going?"*

- *"We are grounding ourselves."*

- *"Who gave you this punishment?"*

- *"We did!"*

It was clear to see that there was definitely a big problem here!

- *"Are you grounding yourselves without anyone telling you to do so?! What did you both do to get yourselves grounded?"*

- *"Well... It's just... we were playing in the other room... and the mattress caught fire."*

In complete shock, we ran to the back room where an extra mattress was kept, only to find it on fire! A mere drizzle of water extinguished the fire, but it could have easily spread and been catastrophic.

- *"Explain what happened!"*

- *"We were playing with a box of matches, I (Tiago) flicked the matches and they flew like gun shots... one ended up falling on the mattress."*

- *"Tiago: you have been burned all over your body from fire, and still you want to play with matches!?"*

- ....

- *"Didn't you see the danger you two were in? And you should always stay away from anywhere that you see fire."*

Low faces, *"Now go get some rest and think about the disaster that could have been if we weren't at home".*

1978: SÃO PAULO - RUA ARIZONA

Two years passed, and finally the family left that house where lived the unbearable landlady. Around October 1978 they moved to 146 Arizona Road. It was at this address that one of the most joyful periods in the life of Tiago and his siblings began.

'Rua Arizona', in *Brooklin*, was a kind of incubator for countless friendships that live on to this day. Some became part of the family and are considered cousins or nephews. One was his friend Gustavo Issas, who is now a dentist:

"My name is Gustavo, but I was known as "Dwarf " to Tiago. I don't remember exactly what year it was, but it was the day the Amorim family moved to Rua Arizona. I was just a boy at the time, I was playing in the street with Dogival when a moving truck pulled up outside the house in front of us. Of course, being curious children, we went to see who had arrived. We noticed Tiago, who's burns caused us a certain confusion, but he was filled with so much energy and life that we soon forgot about that. Almost immediately we began to play. We ran and kicked ball, and in all this excitement... moments later, Tiago broke his arm. You were a beast, it was no wonder, and on a moving day! Off to hospital they went. Tiago returned a few hours later with his arm in a cast and we started playing again as if nothing had happened."

Tiago was always very well treated at hospital during the period of his reconstructive surgeries, and by a great medical team, including a professor who was an expert concerning burns and corrective plastic surgery. After what felt like a lifetime of plastic surgeries and skin grafts, being in hospitals began to feel very oversaturated for Tiago. Above all, he was tired of the continual anesthesia. The hospital called to arrange another intervention, and of course, we took him. We were always very well received by all the professionals there, they all knew Tiago and played with him often. We went to visit him in the afternoons, and a few days or a week later, he'd return home. This was repeated every few months to consolidate what had been done, and to restore, when possible, other areas of his body.

One fine day, Tiago turned around and said that he didn't want any more operations because he was sick of the anesthesia and sick of staying in hospital. We tried to convince him that it was for his own good. He still needed to correct more areas of his body, such as his ear, parts of his face, legs and other areas. But Tiago had already made up his mind – he was done with all of it.

Soon after he made that decision, he was summoned to hospital again – and taken there. He went in the afternoon, slept overnight, and the following day had to undergo a procedure early in the morning. The doctors asked: *"How have you been Tiago? All right?"* Tiago: *"I think I have a little cold."*

He didn't have a cold, nothing even close! He had heard that anaesthetising someone with the flu was something that doctors did not do! The doctors chose not to operate on him that day, and called Gabriela to come and pick him up.

The next time he was taken there, he left the hospital of his own free will. Alone, he made his way to the home of one of the many friends he had made in the area, Gustavo Abissamra Issas – who remembers that day:

"One day, early in the morning I heard Tiago shouting my nickname: ANÃOOO… We never used the doorbell, I went down to see what he wanted, and he said:

- I'm hungry!

I replied: - Come in, I'll go to ask my mother to prepare something.

We went in and I told my mother that we wanted to eat. It was early in the morning, so she gave us bread with something, and milk with coffee! When we were eating, she asked Tiago: - Wait, where were you? What happened?

We were neighbours, I lived in Arizona 246, so she thought something might have happened.

And Tiago, smiling, said: - I was in the hospital ready to have plastic surgery, but I don't want to be operated on anymore! So, I ran away from there.

We were amazed at his response, and well, my mother was terrified!

"Your parents are going to kill me." She said.

We continued trying to convince him of how necessary it was to continue the treatment… It was in vain.

The next time we went back to the hospital, he spent the night again. The very next day, as he was waiting to be transported to the operating theatre, he sat up from the stretcher and ever-so confidently told everyone that he had been discharged. This was not true, but he managed to convince everyone! Early that morning, his sister Helena opened the front door to leave for work and came face to face with Tiago. He was half hidden, wearing the grey hospital pajamas, barefoot and almost crying – pleading with Helena not say anything to Dad. He told his sister that he had fled the hospital and walked all the way home, alone. He went to bed and fell asleep immediately. When we caught wind of the situation, we went to see him in bed and did nothing more than comfort him. The hospital was at *Av. Brigadeiro Luiz António*. From there, the house on *Rua Arizona* was more than five kilometers away. He covered all that distance, early in the morning and barefoot for the second time. He was 11 years old at the time, and already the master of his own life.

We went to speak to the doctors who unanimously said, that if he did not want to be operated on, then they wouldn't do it either. *"Maybe someday he will feel the need, and then we will continue."* There was no someday. He never had an operation related to those injuries again. He was satisfied to continue his life with the marks that later earned him the nickname they gave him when he started to fly: COBRA. Cobra means snake in Portuguese, and Cobra, well, because his skin looked like that of a snake, and he would cut through the skies at inhuman speeds.

After the first surgeries, with the left shoulder healing.
He later wrote:
"Your body is God's gift to your spirit, take good care of it
and give thanks for everything, Karma is the lesson."

The new house was located at the top of *Rua Arizona*. The adjacent houses were expropriated by the City Hall, to be knocked down as part of plans to expand the *Avenida Águas Espraiadas (Highway)*. While the plans took longer than anticipated, the much-desired shelter was occupied by several squatting families living in each of the houses. All extremely humble and modest residents who never made a fuss.

Shortly after moving in, Tiago had already made several friends along this street: Carlinhos, Felipe and Dogival. All people of simple means, and all real friendships that lasted a lifetime. Later,

Tiago invited many of these friends to work with him, every one of them were always considered as brothers.

Unfortunately, Dogival passed away a few years before Tiago. He died in a traffic accident which left Tiago very upset. He worked as a bicycle pizza delivery guy, and had previously won a mountain biking championship in São Paulo. One day he was hit by a truck while working. Knowing that he had been giving part of his salary to his poor mother, Tiago went to visit the lady and handed her an envelope.

Dogival was a smart and friendly guy, who loved to play guitar. He is remembered with tears of sadness and joy. Tiago and some friends would always got together to play instruments. Always without taking any classes, as with most of the things he did, Tiago would just learn on the spot. Playing with the guitar and figuring it out himself, he always managed to pick anything up that caught his creative gaze.

Renato Consorte, today a respected musician and great friend of the family, allowed Tiago to live in a small apartment of his when we, (the parents) were in Portugal. He stated that they complimented and respected each other, and went on to say:

"Tiago had a special talent and was excellent musically. He could play anything, mostly guitar. Despite having difficulties with his fingers, he still managed to play beautifully. His intelligence and willpower enabled him to do as he pleased. We recorded some things... we had a lot of fun... It was always the coolest thing, to just play freely. He always lifted your spirits and had a solution for everything...

Dogival would play the guitar, Mário the drums, and Tiago, well, he just played everything."

All of his life he never left his guitar, and he had a natural gift for playing it just like his brother Jorge. This is what Nuno Mindelis wrote about Jorge:

"I was born in August 1957. (I didn't ask anyone, but it happened, so I took advantage and stayed a while). At the time, I thought Earth was a good idea. I think I stayed in Luanda for ten years, meaning it was in 1967 that we went there. I don't remember the year I met Jorge for sure. I remember I was 15 and he was 16 at the height of our friendship. I think, therefore, at most I met him at 13 or 14. So, it would have been 1970 (or 69), I believe.

For a short but intense period, we carried our guitars together everywhere we went, which at that age seemed like an eternity. I remember thinking of him as my best friend (I don't know if he felt the same, because he was very smart and way more mature than me; I was "the kid") but I felt that way, and I was very sad when they went to Lourenço Marques because I would be without my best friend. Jorge was surprised when he met me because of my skill with a guitar. I especially remember that he really liked a Paul McCartney album (the first solo album after he left the Beatles) that was called," McCartney" (which I still consider to be his best record by the way). If I'm not mistaken, Jorge is the one who showed me this record, and when we met the following day, I had learned how to play one of the more complex songs, which happened to be one of his favourites (That Would Be Something) and his jaw dropped! He was so happy (musicians don't usually get happy when others are good, there is an ego and a stupid perception of competition, unless they are smart which was his case). Jorge was a writer. What impressed me most was that he

37

did not copy others, at least when in the learning phase as all kids usually do. He made his own songs."

I see you running / I see you feeling /
But I don't see you making love to me tonight
Once again you ran
Over the sand on the beach
But when the sun laid away
You stopped running forever

"I may have forgotten and mixed up a few words, but this was his song. I know the melody too. He listened to a band, Pop Five Music Incorporated. I think they are from Porto and they were good. They had a successful song called "Orange". I remember receiving a letter from Lourenço Marques, in which he told me that he played Orange on the organ. I believe he sent me a tape."

The guitar and the games with his friends went on throughout Tiago's life. He was about thirteen when I bought a motorcycle to go to and from work in the city. It wasn't long before Tiago, waiting for us to be in bed, would unlock the bike and sneak out of the gate to take it for a spin! He had never owned a bicycle or learned how to drive a car, but that was never an issue for him, he was a motor head.

It is evident that I always, or almost always, ended up finding out. I would scold and curse, Tiago would seem sorry, but the desire to ride was much stronger; and he gave into that desire often! At first it was only on a 125cc, but a couple of years later I swapped it for a Honda 400cc. That was perfect for Tiago's clandestine night tours.

One of his cousins, Xita Loureiro, recalls:

"I have two stories to tell, they stayed in my head as adventures that I often tell people to this day (as our uncle knows, the Gomes de Amorim family meant a lot to us, and is always in our hearts. The times we lived together were times full of emotion).

I was about 16 years old, and Tiago 13 when he one day asked me if I wanted to go on a motorcycle ride (Uncle's bike... that he "forgot" to ask to "borrow"). After riding a few kilometers around São Paulo, he asked me if I knew how to ride. Of course, I said yes. It was the opportunity of a lifetime and I didn't want to waste it... but there was only one problem, I didn't know how to shift the gears. Tiago soon realized that I was a turnip, but let me drive while he would tell me what to do. I did everything wrong, instead of turning left, I'd turn right, I even drove on the wrong side of the road when we entered roads... At his age he was a better motorcycle rider than I would ever be.

The other story...

The next day, the victim was Helena. We took her motorbike... We rode a lot, but soon got tired of her bike. When I took control is when things got complicated. Besides not knowing anything about motorcycles, I didn't have any knowledge of traffic, or signs, or anything... Of course, we ended up falling off at 60 km per hour in the middle of the road after entering a roundabout the wrong way... luckily, I didn't lose my hand because the ground was wet (I didn't want to ruin the bike so I held it with one hand as the other slid across the ground for about 50 meters). Tiago limped for a few weeks without anyone ever realizing. He never complained about having any pain as to not get us into trouble. The only person that did realize, was Helena. When she noticed that the bike was not in the same condition that she'd left it, she had a few things to say! In short, Tiago was like that, it wasn't his

39

age, or anything that would stop him from doing what he was determined to do; and do it well he did."

Already he dominated his life, and despite being restricted in many ways, he didn't let it dominate him. Yet another motorcycle story from *Rua Arizona*, told by Gustavo Issas:

"We were very young and we rode motorcycles! I had a Yamaha 125, and he had (borrowed) his father's white CG 125. His father's bike had a windshield and that made it ride a little slower. So, in order to beat me, because we were always racing, he would accelerate to the maximum and pass all the crossings and corners without stopping or slowing down. He was truly fearless."

Always in search of the near impossible, but very aware of the life he led, bad in his studies, in his nonsense, disoriented and difficult to guide, he once wrote a letter to us (parents) in January 1983. Shortly after turning 15, he was full of will to live a more balanced life:

"Dear Parents,

For my part, everything that has happened until today will not be repeated. And from your point of view, I don't know how you can still look at me. For the best part, I don't know how you can forgive me for having made mistakes that are often irremediable; both for you and for me. From now on, I'm going to try to be the same Tiago from three years ago. I do not expect, moreover I do not know, if you will believe what is written in this letter. I have said many times that I would get better, and I did not do it. Now it will not be words, but facts and actions. I hope that God will guide me down the good path. I am ashamed of being another ignorant person from Brazil, and I feel bad when I see my friends from my former school already in college, ahead of me. Very soon I will be old enough to live alone, and I hope that when that day comes, that I will be in college. This looks like a speech from an electoral candidate or whatever; there is only doubt about what I can do, but I swear it will happen."

I worked in Rio for a couple of years, I would leave on Tuesdays and return on Fridays. I wouldleave home at 3:30 am, drive to Rio in a great old 1969 Variant, to be at the factory for 7 am. One afternoon, before going to bed early, I felt quite sick. It got worse and worse, and nobody knew what to do. Tiago was very worried seeing his father like that, he was confused, but was the one who took action and called an ambulance. Fortunately, there was no need to go to the hospital. It was a blockage of digestion which ended up being resolved with two fingers down the throat! His immense inner spirit did not fit the body he was given. He was looking for something that he later came to find; freedom.

The Family sometime in the mid 80's (Left to right from sofa to floor: Luis, Chico, Gabriela, Francisco, Helena, Joana, João, Tiago, Lourenço

1983: SÃO PAULO - RUA JESUÍNO MACIEL

In August 1983, the family could finally move to their own home in *Brooklin Paulista*, near *Congonhas* Airport. Tiago was now 15 and had a constant eagerness to know everything, to experiment, in addition to constantly "borrowing" his father's motorcycle. He would go off at night and smoke "a couple of joints" which led him to experiment with more wild substances. His sister Helena recalls:

"One weekend when we were living at Jesuíno Maciel, it was just me and Tiago at home, when suddenly he had a laughing fit. He said that he had drank a wild tea (Psychedelic Mushroom tea) and that his body was full of pink lumps. Naturally, he was worried. He said that he wanted to go to the hospital and asked if I could go with him. Of course, I could, but the condition being that I wouldn't tell our parents, or the doctor that he had drank this wild tea. I agreed to take him, but advised that it was better to tell the doctor what he'd drank, in case he had to be given some special medicine. He said that we should take mother's Beetle, and that he would drive. I said: "don't even think about it, you don't even have a driving licence!" I had just passed my driving test, I passed the theory and the practical first time but driving wasn't for me. As soon as I did pass, I bumped my car once or twice when parking, I was dangerous behind the wheel, I was still afraid, in addition to being a really bad driver! Tiago never needed lessons, he already knew how to drive, anything that had wheels, but always 'speedy Gonzalez'. After a little discussion I convinced him that I would be the driver, and off we went. Well, not only was I scared, but Tiago

laughing the entire time didn't help... but in the middle of the laughter he would scream in terror. Thank goodness we made it to the hospital in one piece, and without damaging the 'Beetle'!! In the doctor's office Tiago continued to laugh looking at me, so I told the doctor what had happened. I no longer remember if he was given any medicine, but I believe he was. On the way back Tiago said: "Now I'm going to drive, you're the worst driver I have ever seen." I agreed, and had to admit that he was the better driver. On the way back it was me who was screaming in terror! He drove like a maniac and we were home in two minutes, with the 'Beetle' intact!"

Laughing as always, he insisted that his sister not say a thing! On another occasion he and his younger brother Lourenço, together with a few more friends, had another experience. It is common to find fungi growing in the wilderness, but if you know what you're looking for, you might stumble across the hallucinogenic or, "magic" kind. The boys had been out, scouring the farmland for bull manure. Why you might ask? Because from these particular faeces grows "magic mushrooms". Lourenço, the youngest in the bunch, ate a mushroom and went completely crazy. Tiago was not content with one and ate five! He got a little dizzy, but he somehow managed to handle it. It was the festive season, so I had told the boys that we would be killing a pig for dinner that evening. No chance. As soon as I called for them to come and assist me, in the state that they were in, they ran into the woods and were gone for the entire day. When dinner was ready, I sat in my car honking the horn until they emerged from the trees with their tails between their legs.

In May 1984, aged 16, Tiago wrote this note to me;

"My name is Tiago, I'm a guy who thinks of the world as the world is, I am afraid to face it. That's why I came to the conclusion, that if death is to occur to me, it's because I wanted it to. I have nothing against marijuana, I smoke it, but I'm not addicted, I can go for a month without smoking and I don't see any negatives. I know it can be bad for me, but living can be bad for me too. So, living well, or to be living on drugs, is the only solution. I hope you want to see this. I say that I'm in reason, with my reason.

I was happy but now I am not.
I love Mum and Dad for being alive for me to write this.
A kiss from
Tiago Amorim
P.S. I do not want to see father go crazy."

At a similar age in 1971, Jorge wrote this poem for us, which only came into the hands of Tiago in 1993, sent to him by his sister Helena:

My dear Parents
(Poem)
What is love?
You who live, who say you love me
Often ask your heart:
- What is love?
- What is love?
You who propose to build a future made of cardboard
How many times do you cry out at night asking:
- What is love?
- What is love?
In the dark sad night
I asked the angels and fairies
If they would come softly

45

And tell me without words
No speeches or prayers
What is love.
And they all told me
What is love
What is love
To love is to feel a bright flame
That burns in our hearts
Squeezing our chest.
To love is to face the truth with your ego
That sometimes shocks us deep inside the Soul
To love is to give what you have, to everyone
To all of those who simply need to live.
Love is knowing how to forgive what hurts you the most
To all those who have been taught
To pretend and not give smiles freely.
To love is to smile with affection for all those
Who were forced by the World
To live in the sadness of death.
Loving is helping all those
Who were born to die and hate
To live and to see nothing but love.
To love is to fight for a real dream of a better World
Against all those who have been taught to hate us
But what do we love.
To love is to give and receive
To love is to forgive and live
Love is to smile and help
To love is to be real no matter the cost
To love is to create and educate
To love is to not pretend and to not run away
To love is to be real no matter the cost.

46

Yes. To love is to love, it is to love, to love, to love, to love
All the people, the whole world, your whole life, always, because
Love is Eternity.

The same feeling, the same search.

Tiago made more friends in the new neighbourhood, which was always one of his strongest abilities. He was the only one with an open sporting spirit, so when the family was forced to leave Angola, I made him a promise: *"One day we will return to Luanda, but we will sail by boat. Just the two of us."* For a while this topic was still talked about, but unfortunately it was never possible to fulfil that dream.

In order for Tiago to develop his skill and passion for boats, I bought a small dingy that was kept at the boating club in Guarapiranga. We would start to go out with reasonable frequency, and Tiago was kept entertained by the small sailboat, which was only his because his siblings did not take an interest in this "wave"!

He became friends with an elderly gentleman at the club, a lawyer, with whom he'd spend a long time talking. He was very good to him, and they became good friends. Like most things that happened in his life, he always wanted change, to move forward, faster and further. The little boat was left aside and ended up abandoned, and the old friend... forgotten. We kept the sail at home, then went to get the mast and hull, which ended up being given to two carpenters who worked with me... for them to go fishing.

But Tiago never got tired of motorbikes! Especially not from his outings up the mountain in São Paulo. He would love to go to

47

Visconde de Mauá! At 1,200 meters of altitude, it had a magnificent climate, numerous trails to walk through and many beautiful waterfalls. He would adventure through it with immense perception. He absorbed it all and spent most of his days in that natural paradise that was still almost untouched. On one of those trips, he went with Felipe Gama; they "flew" there in a car – certainly driven by Tiago. As always, it was imperative to visit or bathe beneath the waterfalls. This time, at *Cachoeira do Escorrega*, they met with a group of 15 tourists who frowned at the sight of a young man covered in burn scars. But nobody dared climb the huge rock necessary to enjoy the view from above – to then slide down the luscious waterfall. Someone had to go up first, but who? Tiago. He looked like a professional climber scaling up the high side of the first stone, and once he reached the top, he lowered a long towel down. One by one he pulled up the 15 tourists. He then repeated that for the second climb until everyone had reached the top together.

Felipe went to the coast with Tiago many times, and once asked him where they were going to sleep that night. Tiago invariably replied: *"Don't worry about that"*. It wasn't long before someone appeared who knew Tiago. They got all excited and asked them where they were staying. *"Nowhere. Let's sleep here on the beach!"* *"Nonsense. You're coming to our house"*. They never went without finding a friend to give them shelter.

One day, a dear friend from the times living at *Lourenço Marques* appeared at the house: Father José Maria. A simple man, but one who did extraordinary work in Africa where he still remains today. The *"Casa do Gaiato - Obra da Rua"* had been expelled from Mozambique by the communist government. Father Zé went to Portugal from there, but like anyone who had lived on another continent, the relationship with his fellow countrymen was not pleasant. So, he then made his way to Brazil.

Always on the hunt for something new, Tiago was quick to call Father Zé, pick up his guitar and go to live with him on the outskirts of Brasilia. He stayed there for about two months, always accompanying the Father in his efforts in wanting to build or expand a medical post, and also a home for abandoned children. Tiago stuck by his side on his mission, without leaving the guitar that he played almost every day.

The conversations Tiago had with Father Zé aren't difficult to imagine: those questions about the mysteries of nature and religion that afflict all thinking minds. The mysteries of Faith. Father Zé was an extraordinary man, who laughed with him, taught him a lot and admired him very much. Despite being more relaxed about the problems of religion that never left him, he still had difficult prospects regarding work.

With the dear Father José Maria

Father José Maria (from Mozambique) says:

"I can no longer remember why Tiago appeared to me in Ponte Alta, an agricultural suburb of Gama, Satellite City of Plano Piloto, later called Brasília. He was there for some months in our lives. I had a small Casa do Gaiato (Orphanage) with only about 20 boys, brought in from creches in Aldeia da Paz, where I worked then. He went with me to the city to make the necessary purchases for a large Nursery that I had under construction not far from there, in Santo António do Descoberto. I then became Pastor there for a year. From there I returned to Mozambique and made a new larger Casa do Gaiato, to serve two hundred boys. That opened twenty-four years ago, and also aided the socio-economic development of five surrounding villages, now autonomous at Fundação Encontro. Tiago accompanied me on these missions, always a cheerful chap, in a good mood for everything necessary.

His face and right hand were shattered from the accident, but he was so uninhibited that anyone who lived with him didn't even notice it. He even played the guitar to liven up a group of friends that he easily managed to get to know at the short time living with us. One day I was looking for him, he was staying in a small guest house that we had at on our premises. I found him cutting a greenish paste that I assumed to be a drug. He looked up at me and just said: "I didn't want you to see this." But I never did see him smoke. I got to know him better in São Paulo, where the Amorim Family lived. He would go to pick me up on arrival at the airport. Driving was a marathon. He would go up the sidewalks just to get to the front of the traffic. It scared me a little but we never had any problems. He picked me up so many times, even when the Amorim Family moved to Rio; it was always him that was available. Tiago told me about his love for cars. His business at the time was renting armoured cars to chauffeur important Government officials that came to Rio. The cars were neat. I never knew of his enthusiasm for paragliding, I believe it is called that. In Rio, people can be seen gliding with the air currents. I learned that it was in these circumstances, through information from his father Chico, that the air currents betrayed him. I imagine that he'd managed to balance himself in all circumstances of life. "Desconseguiu"(didn't accomplish), as they say in the land of Mozambique, where we first started to get to know each other. Be sure that even God was sad, because everyone who knows Tiago, was filled with that same sadness and much more to learn of his passing.

P. Zé Maria with one last hug."

Of all his siblings, his brother João was his inseparable companion. Many nights he'd get together with his brother and

51

some friends from *Brooklin,* in a bar they knew very well. They were friendly with the owner, for nothing more than to have a laugh. One night, a Fiat 147 parked at the door, and a half-drunk man got out and asked for a beer. Upon leaving, the man struggled to start the car. Tiago, with his taste and ease for mechanics, asked the guy to open the hood of the car and saw that there was some simple issue to resolve. He asked the guy for the car keys to try it out. The car started and Tiago went around the block. The drunken man thought he was being robbed and began screaming hysterically when a police patrol car just happened to be passing by. *"They stole my car; they stole my car!"*.

Tiago's friends told the police what had happened, and that he just went around the block to see if everything was in order. The conversation still wasn't over when Tiago pulled up and parked behind the police car. The drunken man screamed again, pointing at Tiago: *"It was him; it was him."*

As always with drunks, it was a stupid discussion which resulted in everyone being taken to the police station. I soon received a call from one of the friends who told me what had happened, and in a few minutes, I was also at the police station. There was an investigator working, who happened to be the father of a boy whom I'd previously given a lot of work to – a polite and friendly young man, who I was well acquainted with. When the inspector saw me, he pulled me aside and said quietly, that the problem was complicated. *"Tiago had stolen a car"*, but if I were to give him three thousand dollars, everything would be solved.

Madness! Tiago was capable of doing a lot of crazy things, but he would never steal anything; he had done nothing! Just a little spin around the block! I heard his voice calling for me, coming from somewhere inside the police station. He called out to say that everything was resolved! The deputy soon realized that anyone who steals a car, does not return with it and park directly behind the police.

All I had to say to the inspector was: *"You never speak to me again. I should tell the deputy what you just tried to do! Just know that I don't like muggers. But tell your son that since he is not like his father, I will continue to give him work."*

At the police station everything was a joke. The drunk happened to be the personal driver for a couple, in charge of taking the children to and from school. Not to drive around drunk of his own accord. He was fired almost immediately!

Two or three houses up from the Amorim residence, lived Cecília and her family. In 1987, her grandmother died at that house and everyone in their family was disoriented and were left not knowing what to do. *"Tiago, in his sensitive and polite way, helped us a lot by taking the lead in some decisions."*

As mentioned, Tiago always had an immense difficulty in studying. Burdened by his dyslexia, we transferred him from school to school, but he hardly progressed. He worked a little with me from time to time, but as always, he did what he wanted to do and not what he was told to do. Obviously, this did not work out, and he had to look for other alternatives.

1988: LONDON

As soon as Tiago turned 21, it was decided that it would be a good idea to send him to London. His sister Helena had been living there a while, and was recently married. Perhaps she could lend a hand, help him start working, teach him English and overall, he could gain more life experience.

We found the cheapest airline ticket, instead of being an expensive "one way" by Varig, it was cheaper to get a return flight with Air Canada, even though they knew he wouldn't use the return. The layover in Toronto would take quite a few hours. With his delicate way of relating to anyone, even strangers, he befriended a couple on the first flight, and managed to tag-along with them to see the Niagara Falls! They travelled about 140 kilometers, which was just enough time to return and continue his journey to London. Tiago always said that he had very much enjoyed his "stay" in Canada!

He arrived in London on November 1988. The fact that he didn't speak a word of English made no difference at all. He managed to get his first job at a Wimpy fast-food restaurant in central London. They had him doing the more humble jobs, like sweeping and washing the kitchen, but that didn't bother him. He was forced to wear red overalls, which was the house uniform; he would joke about that, because he made fun of everything. He stayed at Helena's home in Putney for the first week or so of being there.

In London, with his sister Helena

It was a perfect winter. On a night when the snow was in the mood to fall, when returning home, he saw a beautiful girl in an Underground station. She was struggling to carry a heavy suitcase. She tells us:

I wanted to write to you to say what a remarkable person Tiago was, and how I remember him. I was returning to Putney from Scotland. I think it was the late 80s, and a very cold winter. It was late in the day and snowy outside. I was alone on the tube from Earls Court to Putney and I had a very large suitcase. When I got off the train at Putney with my case, a young man in a coat, hat, scarf and gloves came up to me and asked if he could help me. He very kindly offered to carry the case for me, all the way back to my house. He seemed so polite and friendly that I was happy to be accompanied by him. It was quite a distance to the house, he talked to me about his family, and Brazil, telling me his name was Tiago and that he had a sister in London. I invited him in to the house for coffee and we had a really nice meeting. When he took off the scarf, gloves and hat he was wearing, I was able to see that he had some bad injuries and he explained that he had been burned as a child. I remember thinking that he must have suffered a lot and I felt sorry for him. However, at the same time I was impressed by his sense of humour and openness, and that despite everything he seemed to be a very cheerful person with a sense of adventure. It was from his act of kindness to a stranger that I came to know your family, and it has been a pleasure to meet everybody through Tiago.

As time went on for Tiago in London, he was able to get a job as a courier, and he loved tearing around London on a bike, but as fate would have it, he received a bad injury to his leg when he was knocked down. I remember visiting him in hospital and although he must have been in pain, he was still friendly and cheerful. He recovered from this injury and it is fantastic to think that he was able to do the speedfly sport and have such an active life later on.

As you know, after the accident he got into some greater difficulty en route to the UK from Brazil. The next couple of years in the UK were very challenging for him and I think that it was his ability to make relationships (for example with the priest) that allowed him to get through the experience and build a very positive life for himself afterwards.

I know that Tiago did not always make the best decisions when he was a younger man, but his love for life and his determination to enjoy everything, despite adversity, made him somebody to be truly admired. I think that now, although he is not here, he reminds me to be strong, and has taught me that even if things go against you, you can overcome them and there is always something new in life to be discovered and enjoyed.

I know it will be very sad for you that he is not here, especially having lost your eldest son before, but I think Tiago found his happiness in life, which many people never do, and it was a privilege for me to know such a fine and brave person.

With lots of love and best wishes for 2016, Hazel xxx

Hazel, a great person who became friends with the whole family.

After spending the initial days at his sister's house, Tiago moved into a shared house with a Portuguese woman, Lucy Cordeiro, who was a colleague of Helena. She had agreed to rent with another friend who had backed out at the last minute. The rent for one person was too high, so Helena suggested that Tiago share the house with her.

His great friend Lucy

Lucy being native to Portugal, carried a strong accent. She was always so friendly and cheerful. She recalls these memories:

"We used to laugh a lot at home... tired of working so hard after those long shifts... he loved a "hot and cold" ice cream that they sold in places like "Burger King" at the time, and there we'd both go, to taste that delicious ice cream/sorbet. He would say, "Damn Lucy, how delicious."

I also remember that he always used to make fun of my Portuguese accent, "Lucy, what is this, how do you guys even talk? "Flush the toilet"!!! And "bubble gum"!!! in Portuguese were hilarious to him!!! Wow!!! hahaha.... I miss him!"

He stayed with Lucy for a short time, the house was quite far from London and it was more difficult to find work. He managed to find a room at a YMCA in central London. There he would share with his new roomie, Felipe Carlier. They didn't know each other to begin with, and even though they were two guys living together, they always seemed to get along. With Tiago expanding on his joy for living and devouring those ice creams, which he'd buy in bulk packages of one or two kilos, he and Filipe would become good friends.

One day they both decided to go and buy a bicycle each, to ride around London with ease. As can be expected, Tiago did not just "ride with ease"; he raced. Riding calmly was not for him, there had to be speed and emotion in whatever he could accelerate with! Standing up tall, cycling along on one of these "rides", he didn't see a car coming from the opposite direction and they had a head-on collision! Tiago flew off the bike and hit the floor pretty hard, he was bleeding from somewhere on his face. The nervous driver got out of his car to see the bike on the floor and Tiago next to it. With all those burn marks the became more distressed, convinced that he had caused these injuries to the poor cyclist. Tiago just laughed, telling the driver that it was nothing, and the man watched in shock as he got up and cycled off as if nothing had happened.

Sometime after he'd finished working at Wimpy, he got a job serving guests in a hotel restaurant. He was soon sent to the kitchen to be hidden away from the guests, as some were bothered by his appearance. They didn't deem it right, that a man who bore such

59

scarring would be allowed to work in customer service. At first, even the head chef did not take kindly to him, fearing that he would be a competitor to take his position! But Tiago was given the task of "general cleaning", washing floors, dishes, pots, etc. The battle with the kitchen floor, soiled by years of staining, was near impossible to clean, and physically tired him a lot because of his disability. High spirited as always, he went to talk to the manager. He explained that this job was insane, and that he could do it in a few minutes if they'd buy a jet washer! The manager was reluctant, but she accepted the idea and the machine was bought. The kitchen was cleaned impeccably and instantaneously. Floor, walls, pots, pans everything was like new! The manager was dazzled and promoted him immediately!

It is evident from the beginning that this was no job for Tiago. With a bit of change in his pocket, he upgraded from his bicycle and bought a motorbike to begin work as a courier. The riding practice was acquired with his many motorbikes in Brazil, but some say he was born with it. He never did learn to ride a bicycle, motorbike, car… everything he did looked like he'd been doing it for years. He bought a Suzuki 125cc RG Gamma, a racing bike with a two-stroke engine, that could out-perform many 250's and even some 500's! As he did not have a license, the bike was required to have a large L (Learner plate) sticker on the back – necessary to alert other drivers on the road that he'd had minimal practice and should be driving slowly. A few days later, he thought that the L plate didn't concern him anymore, so he threw it away. Driver's license? Never had one! Neither in England nor in Brazil!

It was difficult for Tiago to ride slowly on that bike, he found great pleasure in riding it! As usual he would push the limits of the bike, and the law, and ended up getting stopped by the police. When asked to present his driver's license, he reached for a document that was the Brazilian CPF (the taxpayer card) that the policeman must have interpreted as a Brazilian driver's license! Regarding the matter of him travelling at high speeds, he argued that he was racing back home because he remembered that he'd left the iron on! The policeman released him and even told him to go quickly because it could cause a fire!

That Suzuki was a beast, and Tiago took full advantage of all its power. Another day, he flew straight by the police again, only this time the policeman mounted his powerful BMW 1000cc to chase the "escaping criminal". The poor policeman was trying to catch up to him, but couldn't even get close. They both ran through the city without reducing the distance between them until they entered a road that had a patrol car further on. This time, Tiago was forced to stop. When the "pursuer" arrived and commented that he had been following him for many miles, he was jeered at by his colleagues! How was it possible that such a powerful motorbike couldn't catch up to a 125cc "motorbike"? Again, Tiago left without a fine after a good chat with the police officers.

To speed up the courier work, he'd spend hours studying the London street maps. Within no time he knew the city better than any of his colleagues. Besides always riding at a speed that no one could keep up with, he started making more money than his colleagues who had been in the profession for a lot longer than him. He was the fastest delivery man in the company, so when it came to deliveries outside of London, some a hundred or more miles away, Tiago did it in half the time than anyone else could.

He soon left the YMCA and went to live in a squat. Squats are vacant properties in London, generally occupied by low-income groups. With him, went Felipe Carlier and another old friend,

Paulo Gomieri, from the times of living on Arizona Road. Paulo never spoke a word of English, so before leaving Brazil, Paulo called Tiago and asked to be picked up. Tiago arrived on a motorbike and Paulo arrived with quite a few bags! There was no way they were going on the motorbike! So, Tiago said, *"It's easy. Take the train, get off at Piccadilly, we'll meet there"*. So be it, Paulo even saw Tiago pass by on the road going as slowly as always, ahead of the train! When he got off at Piccadilly, Tiago was already waiting for him. Paulo took a taxi to their new "luxurious apartment".

The next day they went to buy a motorbike for Paulo. Tiago then introduced him to the boss of the pizzeria where Tiago had previously worked. They left the squat, both on motorbikes and Tiago prompted him to: *"learn the route well, to know how to return. So, let's go slowly"*. Tiago left him at the pizzeria and returned home. The boss accepted Paulo who soon began working there, but on his return, he drove all over London without knowing the route back. He ended up having to take a taxi, spending all the money he'd earned on the first day of work!

Tiago changed motorbikes almost as often as he'd change his shirt, and was only satisfied with increasing the power. From the Suzuki to a Yamaha 250. One time he'd arranged to meet a girl, and thought that a 250cc bike would look... poor! So, during that afternoon, he bought a run-down bike with a 350 engine. He took that bike apart in his living room and put the more powerful engine in his bike. He did all this without using any special tools that would normally be necessary for that kind of job. He instantly disliked it, put both bikes back to how they were originally, and sold the 350.

Four bikes at Tiago's "garage"

The squat increased in population. A man named Alan Maia lived there around the biker times; he recalls:

"I have good knowledge of the facts and events between the course of matter here on earth and the fine matter on the other plains. So, I see this transition from one plain to the other more naturally... and death, for me, becomes less painful. I know that my day will come, and that it will be the right day... Having said that, this bastard had a way of being that makes me miss him a lot. I never saw anyone fight with him, and neither he with anyone. In fact, I didn't know anyone who didn't like him. He has a soul that could balance environments and his smile always came from within, extremely contagious. I'll tell you about one of our stories: I had a delivery 10 km north of London, in Luton, and Tiago came accompanied me on another bike. Before we hit the M1, at Chiswell Green there is a huge, high-speed roundabout where I came across an oil slick (diesel left by black cabs when making the turn with a full tank). Result: as Tiago well knew... one minute we

were on the bikes, the next we were under them... I went sliding with my CB Honda about 50 meters and before I knew it, I was already at the exit. I got up, the bike was just scratched, pumped full of adrenaline, I didn't feel anything... I knew I had roughly a 60-minute window before the pain would set in. I completed my delivery, returned home and asked Tiago to take me to the hospital. He took me very carefully and slowly... contrary to his nature. We arrived at the hospital and we were greeted by a new, and very beautiful doctor. We went to a room, Tiago helped me get out of the leather jacket and take my shirt off... but she knelt down in front of me, lowered my leather riding pants and started to feel my legs from the thigh down to the knee... wtf! I looked at Tiago and he had that smile on his face as if he were about to burst out laughing... then, I told the doctor... excuse meeeeeee... Doc! Me legs are all right! Me ribs and left collar bone are what's killing me!!!! Tiago couldn't hold it in any longer and exploded with laughter. The doctor got up awkwardly, gave me a bandage to wrap around my arm and walked away... For weeks after, Tiago would make fun of me and pretend to take care of my legs just as she did...

I'd like to add: Tiago had already lost his fear of falling from motorbikes, he took a lot of risks, trained a lot and had great skill but he also had a lot of accidents. He was well aware of the situation I described above. I personally saw him come off his bike about eight times. He was made from rubber, nothing ever seemed to happen to him until that accident that was quite ugly, but he'd always re-tell the story in such a funny way, of how he passed the truck, already without the bike, flying next to the driver's side window!"

They managed to furnish the entire apartment with furniture and appliances that people no longer wanted. Roaming the London streets for their work, they managed to find all the discarded items on people's doorsteps: sofas, mattresses, stove, TV, everything! All that was needed was a refrigerator in good condition, and they managed to buy one from a second-hand store.

After struggling with jobs, jumping from one to another, Felipe Carlier, like all immigrants, got a job in which he was given a beautiful Mercedes-Benz. They took full advantage of the car, and would go out at night to hit a few bars, but neither Tiago nor Filipe were big on drinking. One pint or so and watch out! One night, they went out, Filipe in the Mercedes and Tiago with Paulo in a car that he'd rented to go to this party. Felipe drank two or three beers at the pub and then they left to make their way to the party that was on the other side of the city. It was raining a little, the Mercedes was in front, Paulo and Tiago behind. They stopped at a red light before the roundabout. When Felipe went to go, he fumbled the automatic car and accelerated a little more than he wished, causing the car to skid. As he turned to avoid colliding with the car in front, he ended up going into two parked vehicles on the left! They were only a Rolls Royce and a Jaguar, which were now left with impact marks! People began gathering around. The owners, who were dining at a nearby restaurant, were called to the scene. Felipe got out of the car anxiously, mainly because he'd had a few drinks and felt like a criminal! Paulo stopped behind, Tiago got out and took over the situation. He grabbed anything that might have looked like a book of fines and told Felipe to get in the car and disappear. He told all of the onlookers: "I wrote down all the data about the car and the driver", and magically, the spectators left. The owners of the damaged cars then went to ask Tiago to provide them with the details of the other car. Tiago calmly started to pretend he was looking for where he had written it down, but shock, he couldn't find it! He got back in the car with Paulo and they drove away. Felipe very nervously drove about three or four blocks away, pulled over, and left the car there. He went home and only returned to pick it up two or three days later.

One day, real bad luck came along, this time it was big. Tiago continued his work as a motorcycle courier, now riding a powerful Honda VFR 750. On a London street, in August 1990, he was hit by a van that threw him violently against the pavement and a pole! Despite what you may think, this was not Tiago's fault, as he had priority in this situation. He was left with a brutal fracture of the femur, and waited 45 minutes with his leg in the air for the ambulance to arrive. He was taken straight to hospital and immediately operated on.

The doctors used metal plates, wires and rods to keep the fractured bones in place. They informed him that he would have to stay like that for at least three or four months, after which he would have to come back to be evaluated. Just six weeks had gone by and an impatient Tiago returned to the doctor, saying that he could do nothing with his leg in that state, and was wasting away spending his days lying down.

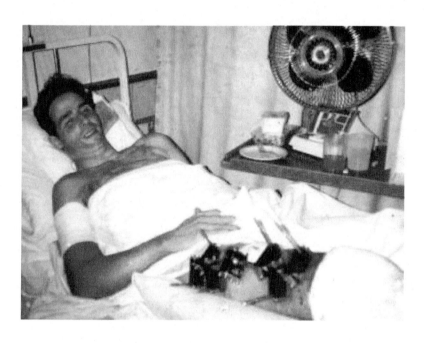

Look at the leg paraphernalia! Phase 1 at the hospital

The doctor jokingly said that if he wanted to, he could take the irons out! As a doctor, maybe it wasn't the best idea to make such a joke. There was no need to say anything else, so of course, Tiago went back to his sister's home and removed the irons himself. Helena says that when he was removing the irons that crossed his femur, it made a noise like an old door creaking! She was agonized and horrified! It must have hurt a lot, but Tiago was, as always, with that same cheeky smile on his face.

The removal of the irons!

That leg was never the same again. He limped as he walked everywhere, enduring pain that never left him. But that didn't stop him from getting on with his life. He used to talk about this accident, always in a good mood, as if nothing serious had happened.

David, a friend and also his boss, whom Tiago never forgot, was very important to him at this time. Some months had passed in this immobilized situation, and when he began to be able to move better, he started to ride his motorbike again. He himself wrote: *"After the accident I was on crutches, still riding and working on a motorbike all day, hard life."*

Guilherme Bologna recalls:

"Remember the first day you went out with her (the bike) after the accident? You could only support yourself on the left side, so that your right leg wouldn't break again. I climbed on the back, holding your crutches for you, and you just took off riding, fast! Weaving in and out of all that traffic just so as not to lose the habit! Haha"

In 1991, still in London, he passed by a junkyard. The owner must have told him that he had a used car, very used, but that it was still good to drive. He bought it for personal use, and for only £60! A Toyota Corolla 30, over 20 years old, but mechanics were a joke in the hands of Tiago.

He always liked to work on motors, electrical installations, and later on, computers too. Nobody taught him anything, he learned everything by himself. The Corolla did very well, cost very little to run and had no mechanical problems. This made Tiago a big fan of the Toyota brand. One day, he even lent it to me when I went to visit him. Even then it didn't have any issues.

In July that year, childhood friends Tomás and Rui Alvim went and spent a few days in London. Tiago was supposed to be waiting for them at the airport, but no, he didn't show! This resulted in them having to go to a hotel, from where they sent him a message via "pager" (very popular devices in the 80s and 90s). It wasn't long before Tiago appeared and took them to the squat. They stayed there for a few days, and decided to take a tour on the weekend and went to Wales, roughly 300 kilometres from London.

The "machine" that always ran!

Tiago always limped after all the nonsense he did when he broke his leg. Using a cane for a while, but nothing prevented him from driving his Toyota with the rare skill that he was born with. The cane would sit next to him in the passenger seat.

Although the car looked like it was falling to pieces, it never gave him any trouble. One of the peculiarities of the car was the exhaust, which was not properly fitted. It always made an insanely loud noise, which was indeed prohibited! Calmly, Tiago would pull over, leave the engine running, open the door, take the cane with his right hand and without leaving the car manage to replace the muffler in the exhaust pipe! Then the journey would continue as if everything were normal. The Alvim brothers laughed hysterically every time this happened in those hundreds of kilometres, and Tiago would continue, unbothered. He'd stop, hook one tube to another and... ready to move on!

He made many friends in London, unfortunately not all them were good. Dangerous conversations brewed, which led some to convincing Tiago to go to Brazil and buy some cocaine; with the full intent of bringing it back to London to make some extra money. Tiago, "selfish and self-sufficient", as shown later in a confession, thought he was smarter than the customs officials. He believed that he would glide through with ease, given the countless scars he had, his limp from his broken leg, etc. Two "friends" gathered the money for him to make the purchase in Brazil; Tiago would be the mule! It was the greatest stupidity of his life.

He left London in late October, spent a few days in Lisbon with his parents who were there at that time, renewed his passport, then went to Brazil. In São Paulo, he was received by a legion of friends. On the day of his arrival, he received more than 50 phone calls and many visits. The next day he received invitations to five barbecues. He was very moved, and when he called his brother Chico, who was in Rio, he wept with a nostalgic happiness.

1991 (END) UNTIL 1995

On December the 8th, after spending about a month in Brazil he returned to London with 125 grams of cocaine! He disembarked with a nervous demeanour, which is just what customs agents are trained to detect. He was pulled aside and told to empty everything he had out of his pockets. They then told him to sit down and take off his boots. The customs agent then heard Tiago say: *"I think I've got a problem!"*

In the bottom of his boots, Tiago was carrying small packages of cocaine! The agent: *"Let me see the boots"*, and then: *"You are under arrest for suspected illegal involvement in the importation of illegal drugs. Do you understand?"*

Tiago: *"Yes."*

Agent: *"What is this?"*

Tiago: *"Cocaine, for my personal use, to help with the pain."*

He showed the agent his leg, his arms and his chest, and said it was the only thing that relieved him from the pain. He said that he had already tried countless other medicines, of which none had any effect. He confessed to everything and said that he knew it was illegal, which was why it was hidden in his boots. He told them that before the accident, he earned about £500 a week working as a motorcycle delivery guy, but was forced to leave his job because of the pain. He said that he wanted to stay in London just a little longer, before returning to Portugal to stay with his parents until his disabilities were completely restored.

The packages were seized, and Tiago was taken to prison. He spent 13 months locked up, and was released in early 1993. He himself confessed, that he thought he was smarter than the authorities, and with all that time to reflect, he had learned a great life lesson!

Soon after he was arrested, he was transferred to a newly built prison where he met a Catholic priest, Father Jeremy Lawn, with whom he became friends and who contributed a lot to his rehabilitation. He helped him to look well inside himself and to consider others feelings through his actions, which he later demonstrated. He volunteered to help the priest with the running of the chapel. He talked a lot with Tiago, and recommended countless books written in English. At first, he had difficulty reading these books, but his willpower to expand his knowledge, and himself, led him not only to read them, but to discuss them with his friend the priest. Above all, he wanted to achieve a more comprehensive view of life, to better understand it, and share that understanding with others.

At one point, whilst in prison, disgusted by the lack of support from the Portuguese Consulate in London, he wrote the following letter:

Hon. Mr Consul of Portugal – ONLY I am here, it's been six weeks since I desperately asked you for help, which I never received, or in fact I did receive an envelope with a pile of garbage. I think I know why, because I am where I should be, in prison, and why worry about a prisoner, a prisoner who is not even registered on your list of Portuguese people! Well, unfortunately I need your help, and I have already written, called, etc., and explained my urgent problems, how I have been sick and I must see a specialist doctor, but I am not dying, I am suffering, I didn't ask to be

Portuguese, but I am, and every day that passes I'm more ashamed to be.

I know that this letter will go with the others to the trash, I will tell you that I no longer expect your help and I don't want it, because I'm surrounded by incompetents, and now to plead for help, NO!

May Sir Consul sleep well and have a happy life, forget that I once asked you for help.

As the contempt for my person is little, I don't have any for you!
Tiago

In another letter, he said that all the support he was sent by the Portuguese consulate, was a newspaper from the Madeira Island, a place he had never even been to before!

Despite writing with many mistakes, he showed a "noble" view of life that characterized him so; just like his older brother Jorge. On March 8th, Tiago wrote this poem to his parents:

Parents
Behold the colour I see, what colour is that?
The child is confused, and punished me
Because I haven't seen anything since I was born,
I don't know if I've won or lost.
My God who am I before You
That in my life I lost everything.
For now, I have you, with that light,
Which guides me.
Thank you, sir,
Because from You comes only Love.
What joy can I see

But with sadness for what I see
Only miseries, diseases, poverty,
That make me cry.
Of course, only a few can see
Like me, when I couldn't see.
To see and recognize, with Love, the creation
Seeing is love for others, as for the Lord. God

On April 19, 1992 he had this outburst:

THE ME

You know, I was thinking about my youth, my accident, the life I have led, my lack of desire to study. Today I consider this an advantage, this lack of desire to study and even lack of learning. Learning difficulties were not due to mental deficiency, the fact is that I was always thinking about other things; it is as if I were here for another reason. Learning 1 + 1 = 2 is good, but learning to strive to always smile to others, to love, to forgive, I have always been a natural lover, a lover of nature, something that is not taught in schools, and is certainly missing.

For what I notice today, is that I, apart from modesty, am more spiritually evolved. First, we have to understand nature with the immutable laws. Then we have to harmonize with it, be part of the natural cycle, and not only learning 1 + 1 = 11. If we waste our lives, that is, the most important years, from 11 to 19 or 20 years old; with our heads stuck in books, passions, bitterness, exams at school, etc., where is the room for the natural ways? If losing the natural way is to become normal; normal according to human terrestrial laws, is this the example to follow? How do we decide what our children should be taught?

75

If we follow the spiritual example, in health, in nature, it all screams natural, something that human beings are no longer. All that men do today is get married, have children; and with that comes problems, and with children come responsibilities, and with that, alienation to the end. Thus, having to return to do what he himself failed to do with his own children, even being the son of his own son, because of the evil he sowed. This is done here, it's paid for here, until the evil is recognized and put aside. This is one of the reasons for incarnation.

I am not referring to myself, but to all families that are considered "normal", or worse. Most will believe it went well, their path, they educated their children, one is a doctor or etc., never went hungry, but is only this enough? Is that our mission for this world? Why am I here?

Even Jesus said, according to the apostle John 3: 3 - "Truly, I say to you, he who is not born again cannot see the kingdom of heaven."

This is, in my view, relating life and death: being born for the spirit, having the chance to return and do what is good to then return to the skies. Or being born here, doing harm and dying, physically and spiritually, because there only exists one death, which is that of the spirit.

It is time for all parents and children to open their eyes, as it is never too late. We have to love each other for our rebirth, we must start by looking at nature, animals, etc. They will always say to love them, I love you, to your brother, love your neighbour, forgive them, help them, but help yourself first of all, Jesus already warned.

76

Thank you, Lord my God, that I was born on this earth in this way, and to have gone through what I have been through, it makes me what I am and that is me. AMEN

Finally, he was forced to spend time with himself. Forced to stop running after whatever he was chasing. Whatever it was, it caused him much anxiety, and such a need for speed in his life. Now, he turned inward, and started to see the world and others more deeply.

This marked his passage through prison. Other prisoners who knew him would write to him, even from one prison to another, and what can be seen in the letters, show the extraordinary consideration they all had for Tiago. Whether they were English, Lebanese, Portuguese and others, they all admired him greatly:

- *Our friendship has brought special gifts for me and I am eternally grateful to you for being you! There are not many who one can truly relate to on this earth at this time!! So, may God Bless and always be that special boy from Brazil.*

- *Thank you for all your help and the time and of course our hugs and friendship.*

- *Thank you for your lovely letter, kind thoughts and love from the heart. I am so pleased to hear from you and I hope you are well and as happy as you can be there.*

- *I want you to be my BEST MAN at our wedding, if you can make it. A very important job for the right person as you are my FIRST CHOICE.*

- *I know that our hearts are always close and that is a great blessing and comfort to me. Thank you for being Tiago.*

He also wrote to a Brazilian woman serving an 8-year sentence. He'd only seen a photo of her that a cell mate had given him; he thought she was a "hottie". She wrote:

I received your letter, what a consoling balm you have poured on my suffering... since I received your letters, having found affection and delicate phrases in them, I truly feel something of happiness...

Of the many letters he wrote, the bulk of them were mainly to his sister Helena. She would always try to keep him strong, calm, secure, always stating that peace is with him. Sometimes he said he was fed up, sometimes he said that the new prison he was in was great. He goes so far as to say that he is taking a *"theology course lasting three years, but that he will only do it for a few months!"* The constant contact with Father Lawn, of whom he always spoke very highly, even led him once to say that perhaps he will become a priest, but in the following letter he voiced his disappointed with the Catholic Church, for its bureaucracy and ostentation. But he would always base his thoughts of Peace and Love on the teachings of Jesus.

In all that time he gained a great internal understanding. In addition to the letters he wrote, he even drew a "psychedelic" picture:

At the age of 16, his brother Jorge, who always had a skill for the arts, did something of the same kind. Once again, we can see how alike they were.

In November 1992, just before he was released, he expressed the following, that also went on to be published in the Oxford Diocese newspaper, "The Door":

- *I was brought up as a Roman Catholic and made my first Communion, and believe I am a Christian, but I can't cope with the theology of the churches. I am interested in a religion that combines Christianity and Buddhism. My position at the moment is to believe everything until I find out that it isn't true, and not to judge. I have already changed. Although I knew God was protecting me before, I was an egoistic and selfish young boy. I didn't give God any credit".*

Finally, in early 1993, he was released and deported to Portugal. Myself and his Mother Gabriela were opening a company there at the time, a good opportunity for him to come and help us. Working as an employee, without horizons, without space to expand his soul and life, led him to write this to me on September 19, 1993:

An example of a day

Today the return guide was finally made because Father has only just reached that conclusion?

- *Today when I said that there was no time to go to three sides together, it was to see if father would realize that there was no time. With that, the product would not be spoiled by staying at its natural temperature. It was not because I was too lazy to go to three sides, although I think it is wrong for a person who wakes up at 7 am, to drive all day until 7 pm. And worse, by the end of the day my reflexes begin to slow, tired. Besides that, I suffer from permanent pain. I have the tibia and fibula constantly together. This makes it impossible to move my foot and leg, but I do it because I have to try to work. When I stop and do nothing, it is because I am in pain. The work is not suitable for me, but I do it, not because I want to, but because I need it, because I've felt what it feels like to be hungry.*

LIVE LIFE - LOVE IS LIFE

In 1994, Tiago was still living in Portugal and had bought a car in the meantime. A used Cortina in great condition, ideal family car, but not for Tiago... In a few days he was already opening two huge round holes behind the rear seat to install a sound system! He put in nightclub sized speakers, but only afterwards did he realize that the rear seat couldn't be put back in properly. Then he replaced the original wheels and narrow tires, for four that he had found with a smaller rim and wider band. And the engine? A traditional 1.6, it did not have the strength necessary to satisfy his urges, so he found a 3L V4 in a car junk yard! He disassembled the original engine and swapped it out. The car choked a little at first, but soon became a beast! Changing engines, opening them up and repairing them without ever having been to a workshop was the most natural thing in the world for him. The transformed Cortina was a success out there in the middle of the countryside where we lived. The day he wanted to sell it, he didn't get more than half of what he paid for it. He sold it regardless, but he didn't get the full amount. Did he care?

Assembly of 3 Litre V4 engine (workshop in the jungle!)

Everything he did was lived with speed, he was a great driver, both on a motorbike and in a car. But it was the time he spent on motorbikes that really gave wings to his adrenaline. He just loved motorbikes. A cousin in Portugal had purchased a Husqvarna 400 2T, "a cannon" as he described it, *"a very good bike, man"*. He asked his cousin if he could take it for a spin, *"Yes, but go carefully."* Tiago shot off immediately, showing off, and his cousin Eduardo Perestrello, momentarily distressed, soon saw that the toy was in capable hands!

In the middle of that year, Tiago returned to London. Back on a motorbike, he would continue doing the same work he did before. As we all know, he loved change, but after a short time he got tired of it all and decided to return to Brazil. He was offered the chance to work on a project that Tomás Alvim wanted to develop.

He booked himself on an Iberia flight without checking the validity of his passport. Neither he, nor the airline personnel could fix this, he was beaten, by a somewhat stupid bureaucratic device. The passport which took him to London for the first time, was issued in São Paulo on 31/10/88. In 89, when he went to Lisbon, he requested a new passport because the other had deteriorated. They gave him a new one, but with the same issue date as the previous one! But why? Bureaucrats must be asked, why they must always invent a law to complicate the lives of others. Certain that they still had some validity clearances, he was held at the airport by Federal Police. They did not let him in, and with only one sibling close by at the time, it was his sister-in-law Filipa who had to solve the problem. She wasn't swimming in cash, but paid for the return ticket! He was sent back to Lisbon on an Iberia flight via Madrid.

The layover in Madrid gave him time to visit the city. He said that he had taken the opportunity to visit the city's famous Prado Museum. He managed to see the whole museum in under half an hour! His style completely. He said that he entered through one door, and left through another, but that he had seen all the famous paintings and was able to remember many of them!

Three or four days later, his new passport was ready in Lisbon, so he returned to Brazil. His brother Chico arranged some work for him in the architecture world of Rio and São Paulo. In mid-1995, myself and Gabriela left Portugal and arrived back in Rio, to never leave again.

1995: HE FOUND HIS LIFE PARTNER

Tiago was living in São Paulo at the time we went to live in Rio de Janeiro. One weekend, he came to be with us, to help Gabriela look for a house for us to live in. It was on that weekend that he would meet Tatiana, an architect who worked with his brother Chico. It was love at first sight. He moved to Rio immediately to "work" with his brother, and spend every day closer to Tatiana. In 1997, a new Tiago was born! Tiaguinho, or Jubi.

Now he was a father, he left the bikes for a while and bought himself a car. It had to be a special car for Tiago: a Santa Matilde, an interesting car, full of problems. The body was made from carbon fibre and it had a Chevrolet 6-cylinder engine. He tidied it up, changed a few bits and pieces and sold it! They started to use Tatiana's car, which didn't last long either, an accident destroyed it! With the insurance money they bought three plane tickets to London, and off they went.

1998: BACK TO LONDON

Tired of underemployment and the lack of prospects in Brazil, Tiago, now with his son and fiancéeé, decided to return to London. But this time, just for a year.

When they arrived, Tiago bought a car. Shortly after, with some financial help from a friend, Harry Cole, he switched to a van to make deliveries. It was in that very van that the couple went to the Consulate to get married!

Soon after that, he swapped the van back for a car, and then the car for a motorbike, as he could earn better money doing deliveries. Finally, a Granada, a big car to work as an unlicensed cab driver. This type of work, the so-called "minicabs", works through a central company which receives jobs over the phone and relays them to one of the closest drivers to the customer.

Gabriela and sister Joana came to London from Brazil, to spend a few days with them and Helena. Tiago, as kind and helpful as always, went to the airport to pick them up. He parked his car in a prohibited spot. Despite the pain in his legs, Tiago carried all the bags to the car. When the car was in sight, he could see a policeman placing a fine on the windshield. Immediately, he started to limp even more intensely and put on a distressed face, which was not difficult for him given all the scars he had. He approached the officer, and said that the reason he'd parked the car so close to the exit was because he was *handicapped*. It is not known if the policeman swallowed that, or if he just found it funny. But the truth is that he did not fine him.

Tiago and his family settled in a mini-apartment in Camberwell. When he bought the Granada, Tiago looked for a minicab company nearby where he could sign up with his car. There were two. One of them was full of "whites", and the other one full of Jamaicans, who by tradition, have great contempt towards "whites" for good reason. But which of the two would Tiago choose? That's right, of course he chose the very Jamaican Brockwell Cars!

When he went there to have a talk with the "boss" of the drivers, he described the office as being very low lit and dark. They must have thought that Tiago had dubious intentions, as the first things they asked were, *"why does a white guy want to come and work with them"*, and *"why come here and not to the other company"*, etc. Tiago, always with his calm nature and inviting smile, said that it was right there in that cab office that he wanted to work. Nobody believed it, but he somehow ended up convincing them. At the start, they decided to only give him the worst jobs that came in, to see if he would give up. They would be the least profitable that nobody wanted to take on, the more complicated routes, or because of narrow streets; or they just simply didn't know how to get there. Tiago faced all of this with ease, after re-studying the map of London, he did all of the jobs smoothly and professionally. He quickly gained the total trust of the "boss" and his colleagues, who started to respect and cherish him.

One day, while parked on a street waiting for a service call, three thugs entered Tiago's car, only this time, they were neither colleagues nor customers! One got in the front, and the other two in the back. One of them held a knife to Tiago's neck, told him they were going to steal his car and to drive to an unknown location. Tiago obviously did everything he was told to do, and when they arrived at a quiet and deserted place, they got out of the car and told Tiago to get out too. When he thought he was finally getting rid of them, the robbers said to him: *"You are not free. Get in the boot, we're taking the car now."*

Tiago replied, calmly, that he would not be getting in the boot, while looking around to see how he might escape. Fortunately, the gang only had a knife and no firearms. He saw a high wall a short distance away and began to calculate whether he could run there, jump over the wall and get away… his leg problems gave him doubt.

After a little more talk, he took the chance and ran with all his strength with the crooks right on his tail. He reached the wall and managed to jump over (he didn't even know how he managed it) and continued running. He ran down many streets, until he saw a parked police car with some officers inside, to whom he nervously told what had happened.

The police took him home, he arrived very nervous and devastated. The next day, the social services were alerted by the police, to whom Tiago had said that he had left the house keys and other personal documents in the car. They came, changed the lock on the door and put locks on all the windows! Impeccable service!

The car only appeared a week later. However, Tiago had no other sources of income to take care of his family. The food was coming to an end, when a great friend who heard about their situation, appeared at the door loaded with grocery bags! And loaded with everything imaginable. It could only be Mina Perestrello!

Tatiana's dissatisfaction with life in London led her to return to Brazil with their son. She was used to working as an architect and having her own income. In London, she did nothing but stay at home and take care of Tiago Jr. Tiago, with his restless spirit and will to live life, had to borrow money to pay for the flights and other expenses they had accumulated while they were without the car. Tiago decided to stay for three more months, to pay what he owed, and to try and save something to take back to Rio and start again. He worked intensely in those final months, doing up to 16 hours a day behind the wheel!

1999 - RETURN TO RIO

So, Tiago returned to Rio with a few pounds in his pocket, the unstable exchange rate turning his little savings into almost nothing.

After having spent so much time abroad, his permanent Brazilian visa had expired. But now he was married to a Brazilian woman, with an official marriage at the Brazilian Consulate in London, never legalized in Brazil, but with a son born in Rio de Janeiro, the permanence, according to the law, is automatic. He needed to get a resident's Identity Card, so, he went to the Federal Police. Bureaucracy, documents, waiting, just to receive a small strip of paper 2 cm. wide (!). A" provisional protocol" from the Federal Police that legalized his situation in the country until he received the definitive card. This ridiculous strip of paper was being used and damaged constantly, meaning Tiago had to go there more than once to ask them to renew his "paper"!

This went on for four years, four years with this "provisional"! Finally, in 2013, he received the definitive card, all pretty and laminated, perfect... apparently. After facing an almost endless queue, which like most people, Tiago hated, he was handed the card and asked to check that all the data was correct, and sign it. Typical, Tiago already fed up, didn't check anything and signed! When he got to the car where Tatiana was waiting for him, he saw that the date of birth was wrong! The idiot who edited it, put his birth date as 1999, which was the date he last returned from London! After much insistence from Tatiana, he went back to complain. The petulant, bureaucratic and inefficient employee told him that since he had already received it and signed it, he could only apply for a new one by filing a new form, delivering all the necessary documentation, and, who knows what else, but more than likely waiting many more years!

Tiago must have been very "nice" to that jobs-worth! He swore that he would never set foot in there again, and he kept the document as it was. While Tatiana worked with her brother-in-law, Tiago was doing odd jobs with them, but he dedicated most of his time to music, which he never abandoned from an early age, even with his hands all burnt and twisted.

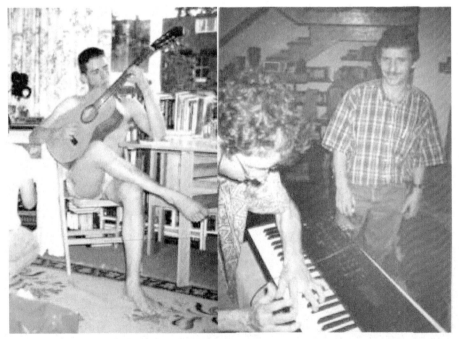

In London   Rio, 1996

2002: THE ARMOURED CAR BUSINESS

Tatiana received some inheritance money from her father when he passed away. It wasn't much, but they decided to buy a luxury armored car, knowing that there was demand for this service in Brazil.

Tiago started by being the driver, which led him to meet some very "important" people with whom he had good chats with and exchanged ideas... which is rare in such a job. One day, his client was an English millionaire, who wanted to invest in Mozambique. As I had previously lived there, the Englishman showed a great interest when Tiago told him. He was very polite, ended up promising a lot of things, left... and was never heard from again.

From the beginning, he managed to land some important jobs. He once drove President Lula's entourage, when he traveled to Rio. He stopped driving these kinds of people, because they paid when they wanted to, and because... one of these, "super important" people, was the main man who commanded most of Brazil. Tiago already didn't like this subject, and after a short conversation, Tiago stopped the car and said something to his face, like: "I don't like politics, nor do I like politicians, and I most definitely don't agree with what you do. Now, please get out of my car, I don't work for people like you". The customer got out. It was only the infamous Zé Dirceu! The most important minister of Lula's government!

Coordinating "government officials"

He had his way with people, and in this profession, he widened his acquaintances in all branches of the Police. In 2002, he would live an authentic police story episode.

Cinematic Police Scene.

Helinho, a good friend of both Tiago and his brother João, had recently married. With his wife Mariana and newborn son, they moved to an apartment in *Jacarepaguá*. As they had very little furniture, his mother-in-law told them that she had plenty at her home in Cabo Frio, and that they could go there and get it. Helinho and his wife went there in a beautiful 4-door pickup, a Ford Ranger. They picked up a bunch of stuff and returned to Rio with the maximum possible load, including a bookcase, that due to its length, blocked part of the rear window of the car. Around noon, a car lined up next to them with four men inside it. Before they knew it, they had guns pointing at them and the bandits ordered them to pull the car over and get out! The four bandits got out of their stolen car, got into Helinho's car, and put the couple in the back seat. With one robber on either side of them, the other two got in the front and they drove until they reached a dirt road which led to a drive way in front of a modest house. Two of the kidnappers took care of the hostages, the others unloaded the furniture and took it into the property. They "kindly" offered the two hostages a drink, which they refused, and then, even some cocaine. The "bandidos" were all high! They all returned to the car and drove to a deserted place, where two of the scum bags stayed with the couple again, while the other two took the car to an ATM to withdraw money from their credit cards. Helinho was terrified, especially because he was with his wife and you never know what the intentions of such people in these hostile situations are. Despite his nerves, he started a conversation with the two sentinels: *"I have some weed here; do you want it?"* So, he initiated the dialogue to try and ease the tension.

A good while passed, the abductees had lost track of time and the other two bandits returned in yet another stolen car, a small Fiat taxi, with another driver taken hostage. The victim was told to take the laces out of his shoes so they could tie him up. The bandits, together with the couple, got into the Fiat taxi leaving the other driver tied up in the middle of nowhere. On the road they passed another vehicle that had an elderly couple inside, and repeated the same assault. They jumped out, guns in hand and held up the elderly couple. At this moment, the four bandits had left the Fiat Taxi, so Helinho and Mariana managed to escape, run down some alleys and jump over a wall into a residence. In there was a mother with several children! Absolutely petrified, they managed to call the local police.

What ever happened to Helinhos car? The two bandits returned to the car from robbing a bank and the car alarm went off, loudly, causing the crooks to abandon it and hijack the taxi. When someone saw that the car was empty and with the loud alarm going off, they approached it, opened the door and saw a piece of paper with Tiago's name and phone number on it. They called him and explained what was going on and where. Tiago grabbed his cell phone, called his brother João and the victim's father. He told his father to wait, *"I'll be right there"*. Alive and active as always, Tiago saw that his friend was in trouble and took the initiative to save him. While en route, he also called one of his friends for help, the chief of CORE (Coordenadoria de Recursos Especiais - Special Resources Coordination). CORE is a special operations unit within the Civil Police of the State of Rio de Janeiro. Intended for police intervention cases that require exceptional training due to the complexity of the work and the risks that are involved (SWAT Carioca). His friend the chief, told him to wait at the end of the Rio-Niterói bridge. He would be sending two vehicles, each with four special ops men inside, and said that he would be arriving to meet them there by helicopter!

In a beautiful, black, armored car, Tiago picked up Helinho's father and raced (and he certainly knew how to race by car...) to the bridge. The two special ops vehicles were already on his tail as he got there. He saw the police helicopter flying in and crossed the car in the middle of the road, stopping all the traffic to let the helicopter land! The chief delegate got out of the helicopter and... into one of the vehicles. With some intelligence help from their police contacts, they headed to where the kidnapped couple were known to be. Two military policemen were sent into the house where the refugees were said to be. They felt more like bandits hiding away in someone's house. Helinho was afraid that they would consider him the kidnapper of his wife, who is white, and he remained scared. Soon, the CORE cars arrived with Tiago in charge! The poor people from the countryside scattered as they saw all these big black cars pull up. Eight armed agents got out with Tiago and Helinho's father...

Huge hugs of relief when Helinho and Mariana were finally safe. All that remained was to fetch the stolen car that had been abandoned at a gas station, where the bandits had left it and hijacked the taxi. Also, where the "nice guy" who had made the initial call to Tiago, waited, wanting to take advantage of the situation and negotiate for having found it. But when he saw all those troops arrive, he turned into a flower.

Tiago took Mariana and Helinho home because they were unable to drive and his father took the truck. There was nothing but thanks for the police chief and the CORE unit. This whole situation could've been a scene from a movie the way Tiago described it... and who knows, it might just be.

In between all of these adventures and services, music was what attracted him. He spent a lot of time and money playing various instruments, almost transforming his apartment into a studio: drums, keyboard, bass, guitar, harmonica and many others. Everything he learned to play by ear. Tatiana would complain that it was money spent that had no return, but he claimed that he was working on a sensational project. He created a kind of Musical Facebook, before Facebook was even taking its first steps. He said that he needed a programmer to put everything that was in his head, into practice. The idea was to connect the whole world via an "application" (nobody used that term yet!) where anyone, anywhere in the world could play an instrument, create a musical piece, connect with someone on the other side of the world, and all interact musically.

Soon after this idea, several multinational creations appeared. But even today, they are all complex to assemble.

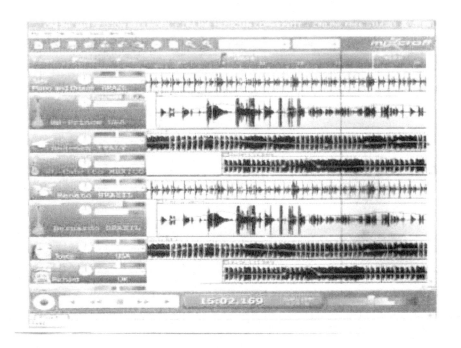

A page from his computer, where you can already see the interaction between several musicians.

Always glued to computers, he began to make comparisons between the human mind and the computer's hard drive ability for reasoning and response etc.

He discovered some videos about the "law of attraction", "The Secret" and others, and decided to take a hypnosis course. He searched the Internet and found one that looked good, he signed up. The course was aimed at doctors and psychiatrists, which Tiago was very far from becoming, but his manner and persuasive power was enough for them to accept him. He was the only one in the group who had no relation to the other professions. What started as sheer curiosity, led him there, where a show of skill and mind control was taught. This made him feel more powerful after the course.

Tiago put it into practice, and used hypnosis on a friend who had always been fat. Thanks to the "treatment", that friend became thin!

Another story, about his son who always forgot to put on his slippers when he got out of bed. So, Tiago hypnotized him while he slept. In the morning, when Tiaguinho woke up, the first thing he did was put on his slippers! And many other times he put it into practice it proved to work.

In 2004, he decided to take another course. This time, the Ultralight Pilot Course in Rio de Janeiro in how to fly!

He was enthusiastic and managed to obtain a certificate, but did not complete the workload required to get a pilot's license. Mainly because the cost of each flight per hour was expensive and it was not a profession that he was interested in. He had already flown plenty of times and was satisfied with that.

One afternoon, with his son at his side, he watched a TV report about skydiving. He watched the whole thing with keen interest and immediately said that he would like to try it out. The next day, he called Jacarepaguá Airport, learned where he could find the skydiving course, AFF (Accelerated Free Fall), and there began a new path in his life!

2008 - BARRA DA TIJUCA

The family moved to a large house in Barra da Tijuca. With enough space to store 10 to 12 cars, they could easily be maintained and kept up to standard for their customers. João, his brother and constant companion, also a self-taught mechanic, worked with him and took care of vehicle maintenance.

One day, a homeless man appeared on the street where they lived. Like any homeless gentleman, he was ragged, starved, looking sad and sick. Tiago called him over, took him inside his home and told him to take a shower. He then gave him an almost brand new outfit which belonged to his brother. It was a "uniform" his drivers wore to work, a complete suit. And finally, he fed the man until he was completely satisfied. He entered a beggar and left almost a lord! A few days later, he disappeared and was never heard from again.

Not long after, another appeared. Tiago also took him in, gave him the same treatment but ended up with a shock. The homeless man had a credit card, a bank account, and they found out that he was not a homeless person after all! They never did understand why he lived on the streets. A few days later, he disappeared from the neighbourhood.

Always in need of rushes of adrenaline, which he found mainly in motorbikes, he bought a Cagiva 1000. It was not a racing bike, but one day he went to the *Autódromo do Rio (racetrack),* at a time when anyone was allowed to enter and experience the qualities of a professional rider.

(Follow the motorcyclist in red clothes -
www.youtube.com/watch?v=5pXwe1ns8Qw)

Even though a lot of the bikes on the track would typically be better for this kind of sport than his, Tiago overtook them all with incredible ease. His brother João, despite being very easy going and calm, which was the opposite of Tiago, joined him on many adventures. He says that on this day, suddenly the rear brake came off! But he continued racing with only the front brake! Always on the edge, or beyond!

Once he went with his son and nephews from São Paulo, Diogo and Leo, to go karting. As you can imagine, he beat everyone. He even received a "report" issued by the company with the best lap times ever obtained there. He appeared in 4th place, a few positions behind Formula 1 driver Nelsinho Piquet, who was in 1st position. In another race, Tiago appeared in 1st place in front of the same Piquet! He really liked it and laughed at this "feat"!

He continued with the luxury armored car business, with the access he had to many people, and above all, contact with police officers, or former police officers who went on to do personal protection services.

Whilst managing the business, flying started appealing more strongly to him.

He sold the Cagiva 1000, which he had already played with enough, and as Skydiving was quite "relaxed" for Tiago, as Tatiana says, he moved on to a wing-suit. Wing-suit is the bat-like outfit which can reach insanely high speeds and enable true flight control on decent. Now that was adrenaline!

He travelled to the United States to experience a wind tunnel, and to order his custom wing-suit that was made for his body.

He seemed to have found what gave him the greatest sense of freedom and speed.

Skydive

The danger was something he never thought about; he was very careful when preparing the parachute, when jumping, everything. And he never stopped. He would go to jump in Boituva, in the interior of São Paulo, in Rezende, in Rio... he never went a weekend without jumping.

In an instant, he was among the most experienced, as always...

Wing-suit

With his physique all marked and deformed, he boasted that his chest allowed for better aerodynamics!

He jumped from planes, helicopters, and found himself going all over the place: Búzios, Vitória in Espírito Santo, Boituva, Ubatuba in São Paulo, Maceió in the north, Alagoas.

Jumping from planes and helicopters had costs. So, better to jump from some high points where he didn't have to pay anything; this is what they call a Base jump.

He explored all the places where it seemed possible to jump from. A bridge in Rezende, Niterói, at Parque da Charita, from Pedra do Pontal in Recreio, Camboinhas, from Morro dos Cabritos to Lagoa Rodrigo de Freitas, Grumari, Camboinhas Beach and Praia do Perigoso, Morro do Telégrafo, in Guaratiba, in Niterói in Lagoa de Piratininga, Itacoatiara, Maricá, Pedra da Onça in Espírito Santo, and the main ones in Rio: Pedra da Tartaruga, Pedra Bonita and the imposing Pedra da Gávea, which would be the one to captivate him. All these in addition to other jumps that have not been recorded.

He would go out a lot with his beloved dogs when doing the prospecting. Other times with his son, who was always fearful and did not approve of his father's flights.

With Jubi not looking too impressed!

In 2009, he thought of another modality: 'The Paramotor'. First, he bought one where the pilot has the motor hanging on their back. He flew a lot with this one but it was too heavy for his physique.

He didn't like this one very much and decided to "manufacture" another one himself. This one would even have two seats, in which he said he could potentially earn money by taking tourists for a flight!

He already had the engine, bought the stainless steel tubes, and even cut off the back of an office chair for the second passenger to be comfortable. A workshop at home (his garage), tubes, welding machine and the new toy was produced!

The homemade Paramotor, already painted and... ready

A welding machine requires special protective glasses, they were his style but he did not use them. He spent a good amount of money on the equipment. The result, he burnt his eye balls from the heat of the solder! He did not feel good, a feeling he described as "eyes constantly being full of sand". A lot of burning and pain, but he insisted it would be over soon. It wasn't.

He went to an emergency room where they had no ophthalmology department. His wife drove him because he was almost blind! When the doctor asked at what level of pain he was in from one to ten, he answered: "11"! They gave him an IV and some painkillers and sent him to the Eye Clinic.

By that point it was already 10 pm and he did not want to go. He believed it would pass overnight, but couldn't sleep at all that evening. The next day, Tatiana begged him to go to the clinic. When he got there, he didn't even wait to be called, or make a record as to why he was there, nothing. He marched straight into the office due to the severity of the problem and the pain it was causing him. The solution turned out to be simple: he was given two contact lenses, without any grade, and eye drops. The moment his eyelid stopped touching the eye, the pain was gone instantly.

Tatiana says that the look of happiness on his face "was priceless" and... he was sorry for his stubbornness for not wanting to go earlier!

When he was ready to try the "toy", he couldn't find anyone who would dare to fly on that "thing" and the new Paramotor never flew!

The Ultralight, or Paramotor didn't satisfy his needs anyway. Not even paragliding was enough. He took a double paragliding flight with Jean and that was it, he wanted something faster, something that wouldn't be hovering in the air for too long, no matter how beautiful the view.

He went to base jump in some wonderful places in Switzerland and Norway. It seems that it was there that he fell in love with the Speedfly sail, which debuted in 2011. Everywhere he went, he left friends who considered him a legend! That year, he went to Portugal with his family. Eduardo Perestrello, his cousin, lifelong friend and considered a brother to him, tells us:

"We met in late July 2011. Tiago, Tatiana and their son came to Portugal to go parachuting in Évora, which for me, was a big surprise because I had no idea of this new hobby my nut case cousin had taken up.

I knew about the passion for bikes, of which we share some stories, but skydiving? It was more of an invention in his unbridled quest for adrenaline.

We arranged to meet at the hotel in Lisbon at 07:30 in the morning. With Catarina by my side, because I insisted that they get to know each other, we set off to Évora. I was surprised by the reception he received when we got there, it looked like "Grande Elias". Everyone paid homage because the famous Tiago "Cobra" Amorim had arrived.

This only showed how intensely Tiago lived his life. Since starting the sport, he had acquired the necessary experience in such a short time, to the point of being respected internationally. I remember perfectly the sense of pride I felt for being your cousin / brother / friend.

He invited me to jump with him which I absolutely refused. After two jumps, we went for lunch at the famous Fialho in Évora and then back to Lisbon.

Every Sunday I go to mass and pray for my Father, Banga and Tiago. He was like a brother to me."

The name "Cobra" was given to him by his flying friends when they saw the skin on his legs, arms, chest and face.

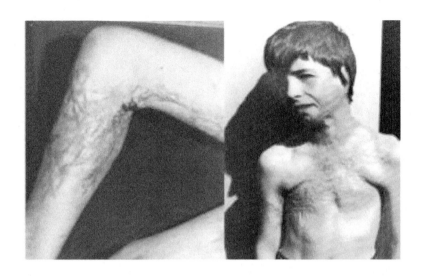

At 9 years old. These, and many other marks stayed with him for life.

He himself would always make fun of it, and since one leg had been burnt a lot more than the other, it became much narrower, which was very noticeable in the calf: *"one is an English potato and the other a French fry!"*

You can clearly see the difference in the legs

At his home in Barra da Tijuca, and later in our home, it was rare if a few of his flying buddies were not staying. They came from everywhere, Brazil and abroad, and there was always room for one more. They would always arrive completely shattered once they were back from Pedra da Gávea. There were so many, that they would lie all over the house, on the sofa, on the floor, wherever there was space, and if anyone wanted to get past, it had to be over them.

One evening, two Norwegians who didn't speak a word of Portuguese, decided to go to the beach which was very close to the house in Barra da Tijuca. On the beach, there was no one around, so one of them took his shorts off and decided to go swimming completely naked. He swam for a good while but was not familiar with the currents of the sea. When he decided to swim back, he was very far from where he'd started and could not find his friend or his clothes. He ran up and down the beach naked... without anything. Solution???

His friend waited and waited, and feared the worst had happened. He grabbed his friend's shorts and walked around the beach looking for him, didn't see him, and left. A policeman later found a naked figure roaming the beach but he couldn't understand a word of what he was saying, so he found something for him to cover himself with. He was taken to the police station and handed over to the deputy. After being asked a few questions, he was only able to say that he was staying with a friend, Tiago, the parachutist.

- *"Friends with Tiago? But this is my friend!"*

The sheriff, who had Tiago's number on his cell phone, called him and told him that he had a foreigner in his custody who claimed he was staying at his house.

- *"What's his name?"*

- *"F..."*

111

- "That's the one. I'll come and pick him up now."

If the Norwegian already had the greatest consideration for Tiago... it must have increased when he saw that even the police chief was a friend of his.

Tiago experimented with flying everywhere. He even took flight with one of his sails in his sister's garden in Itu! He was finding it hard to take off, so he climbed up the condominium's water tank, but even that was not possible.

One Sunday, at our place in Jacarepaguá, when it is customary for children to have lunch with their parents, he got on a motorbike and took some time before lunch, to go up to the Tijuca National Park. There live one or two banana-producing families, who had never seen someone equipped like this. Ready to fly, he found a place to take off from but didn't consider where he might land. He ran to lift the sail and took flight! A small gust of wind sent him back to the ground and by chance into a small hole. Of course, he injured himself. He wanted to call Tatiana to come and pick him up, but there was no signal in the hole. Luckily, the amazed banana growers saw him disappear into the foliage and ran to help him out. He went to the hospital with severe back pain, where he was told that nothing was wrong. The pain did not subside, but this did not prevent him from continuing to jump. Sometime after, another doctor found that he had a small fracture on a vertebra!

In 2013, Tiago and his family came to live at our house. They moved into the ground floor, a space big enough to settle in, and where "guests" with whom I met most mornings, continued to appear! All "flying" people!

His direction changed a little and his explorations began happening in the surrounding area, through the hills that surround the Jacarepaguá lowlands. One time, he went so far into the forest, that he came face to face with a group of bandits who were hiding there to carry out their robberies! With his calm aura and good conversational skills, he spoke to them a little, turned around and left. Another time, he found the Military Police, armed to the teeth looking for bandits; they told him that it was not safe to walk around in those places!

On January 1, 2014, he wrote on Facebook:

Congratulations to those who paraglide; I confess, that I'm afraid, I don't feel safe, they are very big and slow, Zen, who knows maybe one day.

To which Tatiana replied: *Tiago "the flash" life is made of speed!!!*

With his passion and determination, he ended up trying out all types of flights, with all different types of wings.

He was like a machine, tirelessly climbing the Pedra da Gávea and jumping, five times in one morning by foot!

Usually, the first climb would take place before dawn, because he loved to watch the sunrise from the top of the mountain. He found beauty everywhere he went, and always accompanied by his camera, taking beautiful pictures.

He was always admired by his colleagues and helped many to get started in the sport, or even helped them improve the quality of their jumps.

The day came where he was invited by the newspaper 'O GLOBO', to make an almost unprecedented leap; from the statue of Christ on Corcovado! Being prohibited, the company itself obtained the authorization from the administration of the Archbishopric of Rio De Janeiro, and from there he jumped.

Tiago was not a saint. He had done a lot of nonsense throughout his life. He never worried about finances, and unfortunately the world of today is unforgiving. As he said himself, "*I believe in karma*". But he was great at whatever he did, with all his joy and energy he overcame pain and his physical defects. He made fun of all the deep scars and long-lasting injuries left by his accidents. The search for a more dignified life, led him to penetrate oriental philosophies and vegetarianism, and above all, his joy was always contagious.

He wrote this on 27/08/2012:

Our addictions, food (is what you eat good for your body, the Earth and its beings?). And sex (purely physical satisfaction????). And money is the most valuable paper on this Earth; how can it be worth more than a human being or an animal? Comfort, materialized illusion in personal goods, saving to pay your bills, and if not, bye-bye, where am I? Do we have a cure on Earth? Mental reprogramming, install the true version of pure light, and you will see another world, without lies, without selfishness, we are all one, we are taking care of ourselves, and our Mother Earth.

With his son at his high school graduation

On the 9th of July 2015, they moved into a new home on the banks of *Lagoa da Tijuca*. A great house in a beautiful location, with a lagoon full of birds, a quiet place from where he could even see "his" Pedra da Gávea.

His son Tiaguinho had been admitted to PUC, (Pontifícia Universidade Católica, one of the best High Schools in Brazil). He was soon offered a full scholarship, as he was a dedicated, respectful, and intelligent student. Tatiana was also delighted with their new home.

Tiago was happy. In a house where he could host friends, as always, close to the places from which he jumped. He seemed to have found everything he wanted. He had the future smiling ahead of him.

This happiness was short-lived. On August 9th 2015, a gust of wind went against him. He used to say: "My life could be a book." And here it is.

MESSAGES AND TESTIMONIES FROM FRIENDS & FAMILY

<u>Tiago - Written by him on Facebook</u>

"I have no fear of death, death is a blessing, a present from God.

I'm not brave or courageous, but I have enough knowledge and confidence in parachute, it's a struggle between trust against fear; I believe in Karma."

What a photo, thank you Felipe. Seven hours trying, and when it looked like I wasn't going to, the priest swearing that I was going to die hahaha, he went to pray for me in the chapel; thanks, it worked. Corcovado (Jesus) helped me by sending a long-awaited wind; turned out to be a smooth flight. - *Felipe Hanover photo*

Maíra Rubim - Globo reporter

I spent just over seven hours at Corcovado waiting for the ideal moment for Cobra to take off from the monument. Using a speedfly sail, I asked him to fly only if was safe and he told me to trust. He flew and left me with my heart in my mouth, the adrenaline took hours to go down. He made history and gave me the honor of being present. In return, I just had to tell the world what I had just seen. I was not able to deliver what was promised and that was my first unpublished text. I'm sorry that it is so, and that only now your story will reach the audience it deserves. May you reach higher and even better and more beautiful flights. Fly a lot there in the sky, take care of people and forgive me.

At the feet of Christ, 40 years after September 12, 1974, when Frenchman Stephan Dunoyer de Segonzac performed the first Corcovado hang glider takeoff, the Angolan, Brazilian-raised Tiago Amorim flew by speedfly from the south side of Corcovado mountain under the right arm of the Redeemer. In front of him, an audience was divided between those who encouraged him and those who tried to make him give up on the adventure. After two months of planning and waiting for a day with the ideal weather forecast (*"this is speedfly, you must be patient"*, he said to those who accompanied him impatiently), in November, he became one of the few to have had the chance to take off from the Rio monument.

• *"It was the most difficult takeoff I have ever done in my life, highly technical and dangerous. The abyss was right there. It takes a lot of training, dedication and many years in the sport to make this game safe. It was a unique chance and I am delighted to have*

120

managed to fly from such a beautiful place. The gift came at the end, just like in life: the more we fight for something, the more we value and deserve it"- affirms Amorim, who landed on one of the tracks of the Brazilian Equestrian Society after just over three minutes of flight time.

In 1989, Ruy Marra and Bruno Menescal, one of the first paragliding pilots in the country, also took off from the monument.

- *At the time, I, Ruy Marra, Bruno Menescal decided to fly from Christ. The conditions were not good, but Ruy and Bruno managed to take off. It was the greatest joy* - recalls paraglider Luiz Octavio Cardoso de Menezes Filho.

Upon learning of Amorim's flight, carried out in a mountain area authorized by the Tijuca Forest National Park, Menezes Filho was moved:

- *That takeoff in 1989 was my last and it gives me the greatest emotion in knowing that he accomplished this feat. Corcovado is a symbol that blesses Rio and the fact that it is not allowed to fly from there, makes you want to break the rules even more. There is no one who flies and has no desire to take off from there* - he reveals.

Menezes Filho hopes that Amorim's achievement will make room for a discussion about the sport.

- *In many countries sport is encouraged. Unfortunately, free flight is not yet part of the Brazilian culture. The sport is still seen as an adventure without measure and for crazy people. Flying without being a bird is synonymous with breaking paradigms and barriers. Amorim created a new milestone. Maybe 10 years from now it will be allowed to fly from any point of Christ the Redeemer* - he says, optimistically.

Speedfly is still a recent modality in the country and there are few practitioners. Amorim estimates that only ten people practice the activity. Brought from Europe to Brazil just over three years ago, the sport is a mixture of parachute and paraglider and the equipment is an adaptation of the speed-ride, used by skiers to descend mountains.

- *In the beginning, there were people who took the parachute from a plane and mounted it to a paraglider harness, it was a little improvised. Today, the sports are mixing. I met speedfly when I went to Switzerland to practice base jumping and saw a friend flying. I bought an imported wing and brought it to the country. The speedfly wing is a parachute for flying on a mountain. -* explains Amorim, who has been practicing the sport for three years.

According to Amorim, besides having different dimensions, there is a lot of difference between the speedfly and the paraglider.

The speedfly sail can range from five and a half meters to 19 meters and weighs a maximum of two kilos. The paraglider on the other hand, weighs about eight kilos and its sail is 22 meters long. In the air, the paraglider can close. With speedfly there is no such risk, only in specific weather conditions. In addition, speedfly is much faster and the flight plan needs to be defined before takeoff - analyses the athlete, who has four sails, 19m, 16m, 11m and 8m.

At a cost of R$5.000, the speedfly can reach a top speed of 160 km/h, which makes it a risky sport.

- *The sport is much more dangerous than paragliding, so much so that the number of people flying is still very low. The biggest risks of speedfly, are if the pilot hits hard on landing or getting screwed on takeoff. To practice the sport, you need to have a sense of speed -* explains Amorim.

Abroad, Speed Fly championships are already being held, a novelty that has not yet arrived in this country. In Rio, the sport can be practiced at Pedra da Gávea, Pedra Bonita, Dois Irmãos, Prainha, Grumari Praia da Tartaruga, Praia do Meio, Praia do Perigoso, Itacoatira, Pico do Papagaio and other places.

If there was a competition here, I would not participate, because it would ruin the game. The fun is in climbing the mountain and enjoying nature without compromise - says the athlete.

Amorim warns that to practice the activity, it is necessary to take the paragliding pilot training course.

• *To speedfly, you have to be professional. Despite the sport referring to skydiving, this sport does not teach you how to land. It is the notions learned in the paragliding lessons that will be necessary for the speed flight. These fundamentals will teach you about the dynamics of fluidity in the relief, and how to get out of the stolen meteorology. Paragliding is slower, and as everything that is slow, the chance of it going wrong is less* - he warns.

Currently at the age of 47, the athlete Tiago Amorim started playing with extreme sports at 41, to conquer his fear of heights.

• *I was even afraid of balconies, so I went looking for skydiving to treat this phobia. Today, I already feel sad if five days go by without a single flight. Flying is so good and if I was not born with wings, I'd have to go looking for this physiological need. It became something essential for me* - affirms Amorim, who received the nickname Cobra in the parachuting word, as he is better known.

Before discovering speedfly, Amorim practiced other extreme sports, but abandoned every one for the modality that made him fall in love.

- *I dropped everything for speedfly. Wingsuit and base jump are cool, but also very stressful, they make me think about death a lot. With speedfly, I climb the mountains with tranquility and without stress. It is another scenario and although I am practicing a high-risk activity, I feel very calm* - he says.

Amorim says that it is necessary to wait for the ideal moment to take off with speed fly, and that having patience is essential, but in the end, the wait pays off.

- *- What moves me is to fly from a different place and have that contact with nature. Sometimes it takes a while until we can take off from a new point, but the achievement is amazing, it makes you appreciate it even more. Achieving it after so many hours of waiting gives me spectacular joy, it is a wonderful energy, even more so from places where people say it is not possible to fly from* - analyses the athlete.

Check out the backstage video of the Corcovado flight: https://www.youtube.com/watch?v=wsBzFySlwxg

Leonor Alvim Brazão

This week, one of us left. With him we got to know the world from above. With his eyes he gifted us dream landscapes. With his courage, we dare to believe that we have no limits. We all admired him. He was a symbol of freedom. His eyes said it all: generosity towards life, towards others, with joy. He took off, flying, his passion! With him he takes the love that he spread in his existence. Down here we will continue to look at the infinite and believe that his flight is not over, it just changed its destination. Until always Tiago Amorim Cobra!

<u>Marcelo Miranda</u>: Who said that God does not give wings to Cobra?

<u>Joana de Dornellas Amorim</u>

Grandparents, try not to be too sad... I can't find the words to explain, but of all the (many!) examples that Uncle Tiago left, his way of never taking his life (or in this case, the opposite) so seriously, it can inspire us now. For everything he believed in, everything he was and how he lived, the smallness of this transition is clear in the face of the magnitude of having lived with such intensity. Now it remains for us to try to face everything with the same lightness...

<u>Nuno Mindelis</u>

To the dear Amorim family! Tiago, the younger brother that I never had, along with Joaninha, Helena and Lourenço. When I was 15, you were 5, and I would laugh a lot with Jorge, Luiz, João and Chiquinho at your shenanigans. I guess you had to do that last great feat! I know that you are reading and laughing with Jorge and protecting your parents, brothers and son; because you are with the Chief now, but hey, you are a long way away (or not so much) and you have deprived us of your company.

Your parents and siblings are fine, they are made of iron and an unusual iron, but they are pissed. We are all wanting to continue laughing together! Now it's slightly more difficult, even though you follow.

Until next time my little brother, take advantage of that sky and its silent space, endless and so splendidly beautiful that had so deeply enchanted you and fly forever! You are a bird, you always were, a free and very beautiful bird! And give me a touch every now and then. I know you hear me!

Francisca Gaivão

Thank you, Tiago Amorim Cobra, for sharing your joy of living with us every day. For many it seemed impossible to live in your skin, but it was quite the opposite, you lived in a way that for many is physically impossible, because no one has the strength and courage to live so free!! A grand example.

Anamaria Leme:

Is it a bird... is it a plane..? NOOOOOO! It's Tiago Amorim!

Francisco Aires Amorim

I'm not sad that he has gone. I am sad for those who remain. He has gone and won eternity.

We stayed and lost one of the best people I have ever met and had the pleasure of having as an uncle. He always illuminated wherever he was. Always cheering, even in difficult times.

He is gone but left behind many stories and teachings. No more stories will be written in the book that was your life. It has arrived in the final version. And all your stories will be remembered. Always stories that, however tragic, had a tone of grace added by him.

He was doing what he liked best. He was happy. As he once said to me, talking about the dangers of the sport: "better to die living than to die dying".

May your adventures continue in the infinite. Fly free forever.

Robson Richers - Jan 8, 2014

After climbing Pedra da Gávea. The bad thing about hanging out with people like Cobra is, that until yesterday, I woke up thinking I was 'all that'. Then I went to sleep feeling like a Swiss army knife toothpick.

Tiago's reply:

That is it, hahahahaha, the experience will give you the tools to do things without danger, I'm an ass, as you saw. It is thanks to you that I flew.

I am feeling grateful. Mad man... I'm your fan. When I grow up, I want to speedfly just like you!!! They may call you crazy, nuts, loco, inconsequential, etc..., but while they talk, we fly! Children of the wind, this is what we are; and children of your dreams. It was through your gaze, mirrored in your flights, that we had the courage to, with a toggle in hand, raise the flights that once seemed impossible. Impossible was not his word. Barba, Betão, Rick, me, and so many others, admirers, followers, friends and pupils, we will follow in the footsteps of your eternal crocs, with great affection, respect, admiration and security; his daily struggle for happy days, for the pursuit of happiness, marked the lives of many people. Our father of flight, we will miss you a lot. Fly Free Cobrits!

Maria Cecília Juarez

A long time ago, in 1987, back when we were neighbours, Tiago helped us a lot when my grandmother died at our house on the 9th August. With his sensitive and polite way, he took care of us, taking the lead for some decisions. We never forgot that, and we thank him. The incredible thing about it, is the act and the day.

I'm sorry for your loss.

Paulo Angoti: Tiago Base Sparrow Cobra!!!

Alexander Polli: I Love You Maestro

Hugo Langel van Erven - wingsuit pilot

In honor of a great friend... Tiago, a guy with a big heart who will be sorely missed in the airs of Rio de Janeiro and the World. Thanks Bracoooo

Gustavo Areias

It was a magical leap, with very good energy. I am absolutely sure that Cobra was there with us. He will never be forgotten!

Nedson Fumi

Tiago was a great guy and a big friend... R.I.P brother

Elson Alexandre Brasil

You are there for sure great friend, great human being that gave me high advice about the sport. I saw people subjugating him about his precipitation, but what happened was an adversity that he did not expect, he has already made flights with worse weather, but finally I miss him and nothing lasts forever, thanks Tiago, for calling me, advising me. As a friend, I thank you for everything.

Jason Matthews

You leave great memories and we will miss you! Strong eternal embrace.

West Fly

Very fierce in his sport; a fatality. He made several radical flights and one flight from the ramp, in a bad northeast wind, happened the worst; I miss you, you a very good person... Me and his toy at the school... Thanks Tiago Amorim Cobra for being part of my learning to grow as a person. Go with GOD you burnt beauty...

Zames Thiago

Today I learned that the great Tiago Amorim Cobra died on a speedfly flight from the Bonita rock in Rio.

He was the first Brazilian to bring the speedfly equipment to Brazil, he had made several flights outside the country and soon many people were curious about the sport. The first flight was then made by Flavião, exactly on that beautiful rock with my equipment, a GYM, then came Ipiranga, Rick Neves and many others. At that time I met Tiago Cobra, he had bought a new wing and was testing it, we talked a lot about the sport that at the beginning was known as ground launch. Tiago Cobra was a guy of the air, and from what I saw in his accident the problem was in the shape of the sail. Speedfly equipment does not collapse, however, the sport, as well as base jump, is somewhat experimental, and anything can happen… Anyway, I will always remember Tiago Cobra, always with his happiness and his aerial exploits, an eternal dreamer of the skies… I am sure he went to a place much higher and much better than the one we live in. I consider him one of the precursors in Brazil of this very experimental sport. An unfortunate big loss for air lovers… R.I.P.

Blake Wild

Fly free Tiago… sad to hear you have moved on to the next world. See ya around the bend.

Artur Ferreira

For those who enjoyed living in the skies, they are certainly closer to God now.

Tomas Silva

It was an honour to meet Tiago… his unique style of facing life was fantastic… he lived life feeling the best that it can offer… go in peace and fly free.

Djanimal Ruliver

I'm sure that it was not what he wanted; rest in peace, a guy full of health and with a deep love in what he most liked to do, which was flying, a lot of sadness at this moment…

Rodrigo Almeida

My heart is tight here… very sad, Tiago Amorim Cobra is a great friend, I will never forget our laughter with his playful and fun ways, always positive vibes, the açaí after a flight, the reception at the landing at the classes for sailing control, our daydreaming about wingsuit on the São Conrado lawn, advice about life, barbecues at his house, even though he was a vegetarian, he always served us with great affection. Rest in peace my friend, I am sure that wherever you are, the people around you will be happier. Thank you for being my friend.

Alex Vasconcelos:

I loved this guy.

Marcelo Vasconcelos:

Tiago Amorim Cobra, thanks for everything you taught me, in sports, in friendship, in how to see life! I am your fan, my winged brother! Reach now your highest flight! Stay well! Jah will guide you and always enlighten you! Your sincere smile, your teachings and my admiration will remain in my memory! OPSMA, feelings to family members.

Gustavo Abissamra Issas

I met Tiago the day his family arrived in Sampa (Sao Paulo), we were children, playing in the street... We started playing immediately, running, kicking the ball, and at one of those games Tiago broke his arm. His father was infuriated, it was no wonder, you'd be capable of that on your moving day...

They went to the hospital, came back with Tiago with his arm in a cast, and we started playing again as if nothing had happened.

Then I thought: this guy is nuts. He lived with intensity and speed. You will be at peace, what you did in 40-something years, I will not even do if I live to be 100!

We would go out to parties together, meet with friends, and he was always very cheerful. Never did I see him complain, never did I see him speak badly of someone, nor fight or get upset. We were children, and we gave him several nicknames, Caretaker of Joelma (name of a tall building of flats that once caught fire in 1974), little fire, burnt guy, crackling, among others... But they were not said with malice, and they never bothered him, he smiled with us with each new nickname. This was fantastic, he was strong, anyone else might have taken it to heart... he didn't seem to care... he didn't care!!!

After he went to live in London, we lost contact, but not friendship nor affection. When he returned to Brazil, I saw him very little, we rode a motorcycle once, and very rarely met when he was with Gomieri.

The annoying thing is that on May 1st of that year, he was in Boituva, jumping, and asked me to go there to see him and I did not go!

A huge regret, we often leave the important things for later. I will see you another time, we can schedule another day, who knows, maybe next time!

I still have a message recorded on my phone where he says: Love you brother!

He was a great friend! I liked him a lot and I know it was reciprocal, he was always very affectionate with me and my

132

family, we are very sorry! But we have memories that we will never forget.

Count on me for everything you need, I will be available to all of you.

It will be very interesting to compile stories from those who really knew his history and I would love to know them all.

Congratulations on the initiative, thank you for counting on me and I very much hope that you will continue in peace and may God bless you.

I said that if I live to be 100 years old that I will not do half of what he did, so maybe he left so soon.

Breno Zveibil

My brother, my favourite, my childhood friend, I have no other word to describe the feeling between us throughout our lives, even though we live in different cities, there is always LOVE. Love you, Tiaguim... keep enjoying life as you always did and live it. I'm really sorry for Tati, Jubi, Joãozinho, Joana, for the whole Amorim family, and for all of us friends in the heart of the most incredible guy in the world.

Renato Consorte

Thank you friend, for everything you exchanged with me. You are one of the most generous guys I have ever met. A true friend. Look at us from up there... Another angel arrived in heaven.

Mr. Francisco, I'm a musician from Sampa, a close friend of your son. We lived together for a while and we had a very good, happy, musical, intelligent friendship... I went with my wife and daughter to stay at his and Tati's place in 2013. We met your family, which made me very happy, as it was a big dream of his... A person who always taught me to live with joy and quality, with spirituality and generosity... We are very sorry for your departure...

Fernando Fernandes Omena

You made the world a more exciting place, a simple and positive person, I feel that you are everywhere, all over, Go forward towards the light.

Cyril Baussand

You were maybe the most popular speedflyer around the world. That's real bad news to learn of your death. Take care in your new adventure. Fly free bro'

Guto Fly

My friend, I am thankful for having had the opportunity to live with you a little and share this passion we had for flying! You're the GUY and you're already missed! Fly serene, rest in Peace Cobra!

Felipe Carlier

One of the nicest people I've ever met. Very intelligent, good friend and family. I'm glad I met Tiago Amorim Cobra. You're a winner! As you arrived early in heaven, reserve a place close to you for when I arrive. Stay in peace. Miss you.

George Bynghetu

I only spoke with him once on facebook, but that talk was truly inspiring. Condolences to the family!! Blue skies, fly free!!!

Gabriela Amorim

Rest in peace Uncle! May you have the most beautiful wings and fly the way you want up there! Accompanying and watching family and friends who stay behind, especially a magnificent woman and a young son that will always make you very proud. For me, the coolest thing is to be able to see how much inspiration he left 😇 beautiful angel... sleep in peace.

I love you Uncle Cobra.

William Amorim Masheter

He was the craziest man I knew; craziest but the sweetest. Someone who magnetized you towards him, fun, intriguing, and so full of adventure and life. The last time I saw my Tio Tiago was in July 2014. We flew to Brazil for my eldest cousin's wedding and the 60th anniversary of my grandparent's marriage, we had a great time, more so because I was able to spend such quality time with him. At this point in his life, he was a professional adrenaline junky, chasing the pinnacle of human conquest, flight. I was lucky enough to experience briefly what that felt like, with a slower more passive flight, accompanied by one of his good flying buddies. With him it was always an adventure, a mission, or a race. When I got in a car with him, no matter the car, he'd push that thing to its limits - while I sat in the passenger seat crying with laughter... also fear - but there was trust; he knew what he was doing. We'd wake up early and go to some of the most beautiful hidden spots

135

in Rio. We climbed mountains - him wearing crocs, of all the choice in mountaineering footwear. We'd reach the summit and he would jump off, leaving me to descend by foot. What took him 30 seconds, would take me 30 minutes. The man pushed boundaries that to him, weren't even there; from what I've learnt about his life, it was always that way. No matter what obstacles any normal person would see, he would see beyond. He achieved what most of us can only dream of, and that's because he did what he wanted to do - and did it with passion and love at the forefront. He was respected by all who knew him and even those who did not. He had an energy everyone wanted to be around and that many wanted a piece of... and he wasn't one to not share. He was spiritually connected to the world around him as if he had everything under control. Fearless, and for a man that had stared death in the face so many times, he did not shy away, he continued to exceed the limits of his own fear until the day he would take his eternal flight.

I live my life based on the wisdom you shared with me, you taught me so much spiritually, mentally and physically. You are a true legend and your energy will remain immortalized through the stories we tell. Fly freely, my Tio Tiago.

Fernando Brito - wingsuit pilot

We all miss Tiago a lot... And we will miss him on many adventures to come. Espn, I have been talking to Tiago lately and it was very clear to him that you and the jumpers were not responsible for the final editing of whichever footage was produced in the end... he was a super good speed flyer and supported base jumping in great style as you know. Someone to be remembered.

Brad Patfield

That photo I believe was taken in 2012 on exit 6 (Kjerag - Norway) when he came to Heliboogie, he always had a smile on his face and never a bad word. Glad I managed to share some jumps with him and passion for both base and paragliding, he will be missed by many, sad you can never say sorry.

Lucy

I only have good memories of Tiago, always with spectacular optimism and always great fun. Ah now I remember, Tiago came to my 30th birthday party in January 1991, together with his sister Helena and a few more friends. The party was fantastic, it was in London, called "Bar Madrid" on Oxford Street, Helena and I went there many times, dancing Lambada, (imagine, Kizomba was not yet in fashion... ehehhe) having a few drinks and have a lot of fun. Fantastic times. I believe that Helena has a photo of that same party with the three of us.

When talking to Helena today, she also doesn't remember many things, but like me, she remembers when Tiago came to live with me, he hadn't had the motorbike accident yet! The accident must've occurred in the summer of that year, 1991, and we think he went to Rio for Christmas that same year. He stayed with me for a short time, because the house was far from London and it was more difficult to get work... he went to live in London, squatting with some friends and got a job as a "bike messenger/courier" and I think it was during this job that he had the motorcycle accident!

Hazel Cameron

I think that when a person is gone, you remember the essence of them, and with Tiago for me, it was his great sense of fun. He seems to have touched the lives of many people, which hopefully is a comfort when you are feeling sad.

Giuseppe Zanotti

Siete la felicita in persona, restate sempre cosi, un abbraccio, ti ho soprannominato TIAGO LA ROCCIA , UN ABBRACCIO

Anthony McMaster: Best impersonation ever, fly free brother

Guilherme Bologna:

The Cobra... The Legend...

I met Tiago when we were children, but we became great friends in London. In the few years we lived there, sharing the same house with a few others.

Time was short, but we lived a lifetime there. Then I followed Tiago further away for geographical reasons, I saw his son mature and continue to be the fantastic person he always was.

I have millions of stories with him, and although they may seem crazy, because of the risks we took, I can assure you that Tiago was not crazy. Bold and brave like few. As teenagers, like all teenagers, we mediated the consequences or lack of judgment. Tiago more than me, because he was better and more skilled in everything. Where others saw a madman, those who knew what he was doing, saw a genius! Very difficult at times to tell the difference, but I say that with propriety, he was a genius and not just on a motorcycle or flying. I called him Master all my life. And

138

I assure you, this is not an exaggeration. We were happy and we knew it.

We lived with very little in London, but we had a lot of fun. Always smiling, just yesterday I talked to an ex-girlfriend who I hadn't spoken in 22 years. She was very moved when I broke the news...

Elena Evmenchikova –

навторойфотке Tiago Amorim Cobra. онпогибтридняназад. плз,
илиуберитефотоилинапишитепроэтогопотрясающегочеловек аотдельнуюстатью...

(The second image is Tiago Amorim Cobra. He died three days ago. Please either remove photos or write about this fascinating man in a separate article.)

Indian Summer |

Elena, оооо, мынезнали, Елена. Расскажителучшевыпронего. Чемонбылзнаменитикакпогиб?
Будетблагодарныипочтимегопамять.

(Elena, Ooooh, we didn't know, Elena. Tell us about him. What was he famous for and what did he die of? Be grateful and honour his memory.)

Elena Evmenchikova replied to Indian Summer

Indian, яличноснимнебылазнакома,
ноонбылдругоммоихдрузей. почтивсе, чтояонемзнаю - этосфорумовистраничекфейсбука. ксожалению,

мойпортугальскийещевзачаточномуровнеимнетяжелосделат
ьподробныйрассказовсехегопроектах..
есликратко.

Онбылспидфлай-пилотомэкстракласса.
Вотегостраничкавфейсбуке:

https://www.facebook.com/tiago.cobra?fref=ts
Желающиемогутпосмотретьтамфотоивидеоегобезумныхполе
тов
Такжеонбылорганизаторомспортивныхивентовиэкшенов,
казалосьбысовершеннонереальныхиневозможных.
Например,
прыжокдвухвингсъютеровсмотодельтаплановспоследующим
пролетоммеждунебоскребамивРио.
ИлипрыжокспролетоммимостатиХристанаКорковаду.
Илипрыжокснебоскребасприземлениемвбассейннакрышедру
гогоздания... Или... многочегоонуспелсделать...

Погиб, занимаясьлюбимымделом. Обстоятельства,
ксожалению, типичные. Стартвсложныхметеоусловиях
(сильныйветер, турбуленция).
Сразупослестартаправаясторонакуполаподсложиласьикаксле
дствиедоворотиклифстрайк. Умердоприбытияспасов.
Естьвидео, ноИМХОэтодлянеспециалистовненужно

Elena Evmenchikova

Good Morning. I speak Portuguese only a little, but I will try to
translate, but my message is nothing new. I told people who the
man in the photo was that they posted of. They chose this photo
because of its beauty and not because they knew the person.

Elena Evmenchikova

Indian Summer, I personally was not familiar with him. But he was a friend of my friends. Almost everything I know about him - from forums and Facebook pages. Unfortunately my Portuguese is still at a childhood level and I cannot give a detailed account of all his projects. I will be brief. He was an extra class pilot. Here's his Facebook page:

https://www.facebook.com/tiago.cobra?fref=ts

Visitors can see, there are pictures and videos of his crazy flights..

He was also one of the organizers of events and sports games that appeared to be totally unrealistic and impossible. For example, to jump with two men in wing-suits between skyscrapers in Rio. Or jump past the statue of Christ in Corcovado. Or jump from a skyscraper to a swimming pool on the roof of another building… or… a lot of things he did...

He died doing what he loved. Unfortunate circumstances. It starts in difficult weather conditions (strong wind, turbulence). Immediately after he took off, the right side of the sail folded in sent him back towards the rock. There are videos, but I think this it is not necessary for non-specialists.

Felipe Gama - 3/11/2016

I remembered another scene with Tiago, once I went with him to the Nana Vasconcelos show, and we were in line to buy tickets. Then suddenly, Nana himself appeared at the door and saw Tiago. He put us inside the club without paying anything and skipping the line. Unforgettable.

I didn't even know about this artist until the day before when "O Globo" did a magnificent article about him. But Tiago knew him and was friends with half the world. I also don't know anything about his songs, the only reference I have to him was this time in the line outside the club. He recognized Tiago right away. He was very famous, he even played with BB King and Fitzgerald.

Special thanks to Debi Schofield, Lara Proud, Tevin Sahota and Paloma Zhu for helping produce the English version of this book.

Completed writing in August 2016

Note: After writing this book, two more friends, who at the time showed their appreciation and friendship for Tiago, joined him on the eternal flight: Fernando Brito and Alexander Polli.

May everyone rest in peace.

Tiago and his beloved 'Pedra da Gávea'

Printed in Great Britain
by Amazon

84427721R00086